By: Donna Dee

To: Algene

Thanks for your
support. Enjoy the
read.

Love,
Donna Dee

"Growing Up Too Fast"

Copyright © 2007 by Donna Dee
Library of Congress, of the United States
Registration Number: TXu001340361
ISBN # 978-0-578-53838-9

Author notes:
All characters in this book have no existence
outside the imagination of the author and
have no relation whatsoever to anyone
bearing the same name or names. They are
not even distantly inspired by any individual
known or unknown to the author, and all
incidents are pure invention. Any
resemblance to actual persons, living or
dead is entirely coincidental.

Cover art by: Anthony Lewis
Instagram: Vyyae

Printed in the United States by:
Morris Publishing®
3212 East Highway 30
Kearney, NE. 68847
1-800-650-7888

## Dedication

This book is dedicated to those who graced my
life throughout the years and left the memories,
and life lessons to inspire me to write this book.

Author's Contact Information:

Email- donnabolden79@yahoo.com
Facebook-  Author Donna Dee
Instagram- Author_donna_dee79

## Acknowledgments

I first want to thank GOD for blessing me to inspire others through my writing.

Secondly, I want to thank my mom (Rose Merriwether) for keeping me focused, and putting pen and tablet in my hand at a very young age.

Many, many thanks go out to my loving mother-in-law, Devoria Bolden and my loving husband, Benjamin Bolden for always being my rock and supporting me in a positive way. I love you both dearly.

Many thanks to Kim Jeffries for pushing me to even take this book public. I can honestly say you are my #1 fan.

Special thanks to my best friend, Tawanda Cowans. You don't know this, but you helped me overcome some periods of writer's block.

Alisha Yvonne, I appreciate you for giving me helpful tips on what the readers want.

I also want to thank any other family members and friends that have assisted and supported me along the way. I hold you all dear in my heart always.

Prologue

Sunrays shined across my face through the bay window as I lay there in my bed dreading the need to get up. *Niyah, you aren't as young as you use to be,* I thought to myself as my head throbbed due to the party the night before. I'd taken a week off from work and this morning would be used to do a little housework before my cousin, Dana, came the next morning. It had been a while since I last talked to her, but my mom set up a meeting between us two. I was glad to have the chance to establish our sister bond once again.

I live alone, but you would think I live with a house full of people by the way my house looked.

I went downstairs and fixed myself some scrambled egg whites, turkey bacon, and a piece of wheat toast. I drank my usual glass of fresh squeezed orange juice. I looked over and checked my voicemail on my cell phone. I had six messages. *Man, I must have really been out of it 'cause I didn't even hear the phone ring last night,* I thought. I glanced at the clock and it read a quarter to nine. I ran upstairs to put on some loose clothes and put my hair up in a ponytail.

After changing, I stood in the middle of the kitchen, scanning the room from left to right, wondering where to start. I turned on the radio for a little motivational music, which always seemed to get me in the mood for chores. Boy, I had really worked up a sweat, because before I knew it, it was noon. The house was spotless from top to bottom except for my desk sitting in the corner of the living room. I placed the important documents into the file cabinet that sat right below the desk, and then discarded the old papers. After I got to the bottom of the drawer, I found a white gift box with little purple butterflies on top of it.

I picked it up and held it close to my heart, choking back the tears that began to swell up. My hands trembled as I opened the lid. I found a framed photo on the inside, and all I could do was stare. Looking at the image brought back so many memories. As I wiped a small layer of dust from the frame a tear fell, smearing across the glass. It was such an angelic picture of my mother, Rosa. She was such an attractive woman. She looked so happy and at peace. The portrait was of mom holding me in her arms, and we were both smiling. I couldn't have been more than two years old. I leaned against the couch pressing the container against my chest, drifting away in memories.

# SECTION 1

## Old Memories

Chapter 1

I never knew my father. My parents got married at the young age of nineteen, but got divorced right before I was born. My mother was left to raise me on her own. She did a good job 'cause I don't remember having problems until her high school ten- year reunion. I was nine-years-old and she was twenty-eight.

I sat on top of the toilet seat, watching mom get dressed. I couldn't help but think about how beautiful she always looked. I had watched her plenty of nights getting dressed to go out on dates. Little did I know that night would change both our lives forever. Mom wore a red dress and a red rose on the side of her ever-flowing, black, curly hair. She dabbed her neck and wrists with a sweet smelling perfume, and then turned and kissed me softly on my nose. Me, being a pest, I asked her if she really had to go, and why I had to go to stay over grandma Ella's for the night?

"Niyah, pumpkin, it's just for tonight. I promise I'll make it up to you tomorrow."

"But, mom," I whined. "Can't you stay at home and read to me instead?"

"No, darling. I'll be back before you know it."

I sighed loudly as she assured me of her love with a hug. An hour later we were standing in Grandma Ella's doorway. I cried for her not to leave, but she blew me a kiss then drove off. I cried myself to sleep that night.

The next morning, I had awakened to the sound of my grandma frantically running around the house. I sat up in bed, trying to collect myself. She ran in to me and got down on her knees and told me there was an accident. She lost me at the word accident, and I began to wail. Her lips were moving, but I couldn't hear anything coming out. My aunt, Sharon came over, and we all rushed off to the hospital to see my mother. We entered her room and saw her lying in the bed with her eyes closed. Tubes and wires were all over her body. My knees became weak as I fell to the floor.

The doctor came in and said that Mom would be alright. Someone had put something in her drink. It was a drug called LSD and PCP, and it affects the brain cells. The doctor stated that it would take a while for Mom to come back to herself, and that she may not remember much at first, but she would soon come around. After six months of healing from her accident, everything seemed okay, but then she became addicted to the medicine the doctor had prescribed. One year later, we were all standing in court, listening to a judge as he awarded custody of me to Grandma Ella. My mother was put in a drug rehabilitation center. She openly admitted she needed help.

I was angry because it seemed as if nobody asked me what I wanted to do or where I wanted to live. This was hard for me because I'd never been away from my mother for more than a day or so. The judge ordered Mom to stay in the facility for a year. The first night without mom, I cried and longed to have her near me. A year turned into three years. Soon, I started to feel comfortable living with my grandmother. She taught me how to sew and cook, which I enjoyed.

I had just entered junior high school and made new friends. An old friend from my grandmother's past came and swept her off of her feet. My first grandfather died a little over eight years before, and Grandma Ella claimed she was lonely. I tried to persuade her that I was there and she wasn't alone, but she explained to me that the love from a man is what she was missing. Who knew the next three weeks would be pure torture for me? Without asking or consulting me, my grandma pulled me out of school, away from all my friends, and we moved all the way to Waukegan, Illinois.

It was wonderful at first. Earl, my grandmother's new husband bought me things and treated me as his own grandchild. After a while things turned for the worse again. Earl felt that I was taking quality time from his marriage. It got to the point that I had to eat dinner in the basement alone because they were discussing adult business at the table, and he didn't want me to hear. I soon began to hate Earl. I would always try my best to stay away from home. I'd ride my bike all day long. I remember one evening I came in and Earl told me I wasn't allowed to ride my bike anymore 'cause I would stay gone too much. I could feel the veins in my neck tingle, and I couldn't hold back my anger any longer. I lashed out.

"This is some real bullshit, you know," I exclaimed. You don't want me riding my bike or talking to any other kids on the block because they're bad association. Who can I talk to or hang with 'cause I can't even spend time with my own grandmother?' I was even bold enough to put my finger in his face. If you hate me so much and don't want me here, then please send me back to Memphis so I can be around people who actually love me."

"Okay . . . fine with me," he replied.

4

Just like that, it was settled. But what really hurt me was my grandmother who happily agreed to me leaving. She said I was getting in the way of her relationship with her new husband. She even went on to say they didn't even have a chance to go on their honeymoon because I was still in school. They were both old and wanted to enjoy their lives. Grandma Ella stated she had talked to Sharon, and she said it was okay for me to live with her.

At that moment she began to cry.

"Why are you crying, Grandma Ella? You shouldn't have brought me all the way up here with you. I didn't want to come in the first place," I said, full of hurt.

I could tell that statement took her for a loop.

"Niyah, I just want what's good for you. We can still talk on the phone and write each other. You act as if this is the end."

"Grandma Ella, look. I'm thirteen. I've probably had more people walk out on me than some older people have. You, of all people, should understand how I feel."

She just stared at me. I could tell by the look in her eyes that no matter what I said, she was still choosing Earl over me.

Only a few days had passed before it was time for Earl and Grandma Ella to drive me back to Memphis. It was a long and silent trip. When we arrived at Sharon's house, I grabbed my two suitcases and my duffel bag then ran to hug my aunt. I was so happy to be there with her and my favorite cousin, Dana. Dana quickly rushed me off to my new room to settle my things. After a while, Grandma Ella came in and asked if I was going to say goodbye to Earl.

"Oh, yeah. Tell him bye for me," I said sarcastically.

Then I returned to what I was doing. She grabbed my arm, twisting it slightly. "I need to see you in the hall, Niyah," she said.

"Grandma Ella, I'm busy unpacking. Can't this wait 'til some other time?"

There was a long pause. When I saw she was serious I followed her into the front room.

"Niyah, you're getting so tall and your hair is getting so long it reminds me of your mother's locks very much. You're almost fourteen and have your whole life ahead of you."

"Grandma Ella, please," I interrupted. "Did you want me to come in here to talk about how I look?"

"Sweetie, I love you, and I'm trying to make this easy on myself," she replied.

"Well, you will be making it easier on both of us if you wipe those fake tears away and just leave."

She ran out the hall crying, and I went to my room and slammed the door. Sharon walked in and asked me what was going on.

"I'm just ready to get this behind me and get on with my life," I responded.

"Niyah, she's still your grandmother and you should understand why she did what she did."

"Sharon I know why she did it, and I don't want to talk about it."

"Okay you have some unpacking to do anyway."

She closed the door behind her as she left out. Considering all the madness, Dana went to her own bedroom. I sat on the bed and looked around my new place of solitude. It was small but cozy. It had hardwood floors, and a long oval shaped mirror trimmed in lavender was on the back of the door. The closet doors were white and looked like large window shutters. It was the largest walk-in closet I'd ever seen. There was a medium dresser with an oval shaped mirror attached to it. In the opposite corner was a matching Chester. A small television and VCR sat on it.

The walls in the room were painted the same color as the outline of the mirror. Above the bed were two pictures of ballet dancers. The bed was made perfectly with crisp linen sheets and a huge comforter. I sat there marveling, thinking I finally get a chance to be happy again. As I lay back on the bed an object bumped my arm. I grabbed the box, which was wrapped in pink paper with a big purple bow on top. I quickly opened it, anticipating what was inside. It was a small jewelry case. When I opened it, a tiny ballerina twirled to an angelic tune. I shed a few tears as I ran to hug and thank Sharon.

"What was that for, silly girl?" she asked.

"The beautiful gift. I love it," I responded, smiling.

"I didn't get you that. Your mother Rosa bought that for you. Didn't you see the letter she enclosed with it?"

I hurried back to find the letter. I held the small envelope in my hand afraid to open it. I hadn't seen or heard from my mother in almost four years. I wasn't afraid of her per say, but what the contents of the letter might say. I finally took a deep breath and opened it.

*To my lovely daughter,*

*I have missed you so much. I haven't seen you in over three years. I feel like I'm missing out on the important parts of your life. . Your aunt tells me you and Dana will be going to the ninth grade when school starts. You're practically a young woman. I bet you are so pretty. Look, Niyah, I'm sorry I got strung out on those drugs and messed up your life. I really hate myself for that. Things would be great if I wouldn't have gone to that party like you asked.*

*Pumpkin, please don't be mad at Grandmother Ella or me. Sharon told me what happened in Illinois and I'm glad you will be staying with her now. You and Dana are practically like sisters. I know you will love it there. How do you like your room? Sharon asked me to come and help decorate it for you. I picked out the lavender paint and ballerina pictures. I remembered how much you loved to watch ballet dancers and the color purple. The rest of the things Dana helped picked out.*

*Pumpkin, I'm not on drugs anymore. I have been clean for three years now. I would love for us to be back like we were, but the judge stated that because of the medicine I'm on now, it is better for you and I to live apart. Not being with you hurts so much, but I'm strong, and I have a great inspiration in you. I'm doing this for us 'cause one day we'll be together. Well, be obedient to your aunt, do your homework, and keep those A's coming in school. Maybe one day you can go to college and be a computer programmer like I was. Well, honey, I love you and always will. Pray for me every night, and I'll do the same for you.*

      *Love your mom,*
      *Rosa*

      *P.S. Watch for them knuckle head boys, 'cause I saw those pictures your grandmother sent to me of you at the beach. And what are you doing in a bikini anyway? Anyway don't let anyone hurt you.*
      *Xoxoxoxox*

I was so excited to hear from my mom, that I was crying and laughing at the same time. My mom was right. My body did develop fast, but she was late. My period had started two years before. And I was far from being a virgin. I had been having sex since I was twelve. I just never told anyone. As I grabbed for a Kleenex to wipe my tears, someone knocked at my door.

"Who is it? Give me a minute," I said, trying to quickly compose myself.

"It's me, Niyah," Dana said.

"Come on in, girl," I said, wiping my face.

"Still unpacking?" she asked. "Let me help you."

"Okay. I could use a hand."

I laid my teddy bears on my bed as Dana set up my small boom box and plugged it in. I put the few pieces of jewelry I had in my new case. Then we both hung my clothes in the closet. We sat on the floor and put my undergarments and socks in the drawers. We laughed and caught up on old times as we put away my belongings

My mom was right. We were like sisters. I could always confide in her. We could sit for hours talking and laughing. After I told her about my first time, she told me about hers as agreed. Hers was much more glamorous than mine. Then we chatted about our futures. I told her I wanted to marry a nice handsome man someday. I wanted two kids, a boy, and a girl. I wanted a dog, a cat, and to live in a big house with a huge yard. After I painted her a mind's portrait of how my house would look, she told me what she wanted in life. She said she didn't care where she lived, or how many children she had, or even if her husband would be handsome, she just wanted to marry a man who would love and respect both her and their children. I understood exactly what she meant.

Dana's real father cheated on her mom and left her to care for two kids on her own. Dana loved her dad, but I guess he just wasn't ready for a family. After a while Dana finally gave up on her father coming back home. Sharon raised Dana to the best of her ability. After a few years Sharon married again. She married a nice-looking man named James.

It seemed to be heaven on earth for Sharon, or maybe she was just too blind to see he was really the devil in disguise. Personally, I didn't like him from the jump.

Sharon worked at an administrative office where she had to be dress up. She was also beautiful like my mother. She had long black shiny hair and her makeup always looked natural. A few weeks after James moved in with Sharon, his true colors came flowing out. Sharon was no longer allowed to wear makeup or finger nail polish. She had to wear a ponytail pulled back to the back at all times. She also had to wear long old-lady looking dresses. She began to look rundown and tired. One day Dana asked her mother why she let James control the way she looked, and Sharon said because he was her husband.

Things really started to get bad. James threw all Sharon's furniture out and bought what he wanted in their home. He took out the dishwasher in order to make Dana hand wash the dishes in water so hot, one could barely stand to touch it. I remember one time Grandma Ella had to put ointment on Dana's hands from all the burns. One Sunday morning when Dana was dressed to go to church, James pushed her into a thorn bush as she tried to get into the van. He said it was an accident. He was abusive to Dana, and Sharon still loved his dirty drawers. Soon James and Sharon separated.

Later that night after our talk, I lay in my bed and held my favorite teddy bear tight. I closed my eyes and drifted to sleep.

I was awakened the next morning by the smell of homemade biscuits. I slid on my slippers and robe then ran to the bathroom to wash my face. When I made it to the kitchen, to my surprise, Dana was cooking.

"Girl, I wanted to surprise you with breakfast," she said.

"Well, let's surprise Sharon instead."

Dana finished the eggs and bacon, and I set the table. As we were finishing, Sharon walked in. We didn't notice her because we were dancing and singing. We were so embarrassed when she clapped. She came and kissed us both on top of our heads. The next two months seemed to fly by. We went to see plays and ball games. We'd also skate, ride our bikes, shop, and visit my mother every Friday.

School was less than a week away. My mom and grandmother sent money to Sharon to buy my school supplies. Before the first day of school, we went to the beauty shop, and with my hair whipped and a new outfit, you couldn't tell me anything. The next morning, Dana, and I put on white K-Swiss shoes and blue jeans. Dana had on a white shirt with SWEET DEE airbrushed on the front. I had on a white t-shirt that had SPOILED written in red glitter letters on the front. We both had matching black backpacks. Anyone would have thought we were sisters. The only difference was that she was a few inches taller and was darker than me. We had slender bodies and were able to wear each other's shoes and clothes. As we waited on our ride, Dana updated me on the latest gossip. She informed me of whom to socialize with and who not to hang with.

The school was rather small and not quite what I expected. Havenview Middle School only had two main halls and didn't have many students. I loved the quiet and preppy atmosphere. Everyone seemed cool. *This just might be the new start that I need*, I thought as I took it all in.

## CHAPTER 2

By springtime, things were starting to look up. I had made a lot of friends. I had made the track and volleyball teams. Demonte, was a new guy that I'd been dating for a few months. I would go and visit my mother and wrote Grandma Ella regularly.

One day, during spring break in April, I had to go to school for track practice. I was so tired and worn out by the end of practice, I could hardly breath. Coach had us run five laps twice, and my legs felt like lead. After we had all showered, I gathered my things. Linda, one of my close friends, came in and told me Demonte, my new boyfriend, was outside waiting for me. I usually rode home with Linda, but I told her it was okay because I'd walk with Demonte since Sharon's house was only a few blocks away. I saw a smile on Demonte's face. I asked him what he was smiling at.

"You, babe," he said.

"Whatever. Walk with me to the store then to my house," I replied.

"Girl, is that a question or a demand?"

"Demand," I responded then kissed his lips.

"Well, I beat you this time," he said jokingly.

He reached into his jacket and pulled out a bag of Doritos and a Hawaiian punch drink. We sat on the gym steps and snacked.

"Come with me I want to show you something, Niyah," he said.

"What? Why?"

"Hard-head just come with me."

"Demonte, you know I can't be gone too long. It's one o'clock now, and I've got chores to do before Sharon gets home."

"Girl, you'll be home in time."

After a few more minutes of debating back and forth, I finally gave in. Demonte gathered my things and grabbed my hand. As soon as we entered the house, he put my stuff down and covered my eyes with his hands. At first I hesitated, but soon I trusted him to guide me down what seemed like a never-ending hallway.

"This is it. My room," he said just after taking his hands down from my face.

He had a simple yet masculine room. His walls were painted baby blue with navy & baby blue plaid border. I walked over and marveled at his autographed Michael Jordan posters as he beckoned me to sit on the bed next to him.

11

"This is a really cool room, Demonte," I said, looking around.

"Yeah, this is my place of solitude when I want to get away from it all. Kick off your shoes and get comfortable, girl."

"I can't. I really need to be getting home soon. What is it that you had to show me?"

"I'll show you after you let me rub your feet."

I took off my shoes and socks and put my feet over his legs. He rubbed my feet with compassion. My feet were killing me after running all those laps. I began to get nervous when we sat in silence for a few minutes.

"Demonte, look, what is it you want to show me?" I asked, getting impatient.

"Can I show you some affection first, girl?"

"Okay, but I'm not going to be over here long."

"Just sit back and relax, girl."

He knew my aunt was strict when it came to boys. She still thought Dana and I were virgins. She would let us talk to boys on the phone, but they couldn't come over. She felt we were too young to date, but Dana and I did a fine job of hiding secrets from her. The foot massage felt so good that I flopped back on his bed to get cozy. I was so deep in conversation about my track meet that I hadn't realized his hands had moved up to my knees and calf muscles. I began talking about one of the new girls on the team then I realized he was rubbing the inner and outer part of my thighs. He then moved his hands to the waistband of my shorts.

"Demonte, what are you doing?" I asked.

"Relax, I just want to make sure I rub your entire leg," he replied.

I don't know how it happened, but a simple massage turned into a whole lot more.

"Stop, Demonte. I can't do this. Let me up. I have to go."

"Please, Niyah, I love you. And I want to show you how much."

"Okay, Demonte, just be gentle with me."

"I will. I promise I'll take my time."

"And vow to me that you'll never leave me."

"I won't. Niyah, I won't," he replied as he gently kissed my lips.

It was natural how our bodies moved together in unison. Afterwards, we held each other as we tried to catch our breaths. I felt comfortable and secure with him. I wished our moment wouldn't end. I glanced over at the clock and noticed it was two-twenty. I quickly jumped up and gathered my things. I went into the bathroom, washed up, and then straightened my hair. As I pulled my hair back into a ponytail, Demonte walked up behind me and placed a small silver heart necklace around my neck. Before I could say a word, he put his finger over my lips.

"Babe, this is what I wanted to show and give to you."

I thanked him by giving him a small peck on his cheek.

"Nobody has ever given me something so special. Thank you," I said, feeling warm inside.

"You're special to me, Niyah."

"I promise I'll cherish it. Always."

"When you're done getting dressed, do you want me to walk you home?"

"No, it won't take me long to get home. It's only two blocks away."

He patted me on my behind as I trotted out the door past him.

"I love you, Niyah," he said.

I just kept on jogging as if I didn't hear him. I smiled from ear to ear. It felt so good to be loved-an emotion I hadn't encountered in a while. I loved him too, but I wanted to tell him when I knew the time was right. I was afraid he'd leave me once he discovered he had my heart. It didn't take me long to get home. I ran straight to my room to put my things up. I didn't hear or see Dana, so I figured she was asleep. I cleaned the kitchen and straightened up the den area very quickly. I made sure I did my chores first 'cause Sharon would've blown a gasket if she came home and the house was a mess. After showering, I got dressed then went into the kitchen, and stared in the fridge, deciding what to cook for dinner. I saw we had salsa, fresh ground beef, lettuce, tomatoes, and cheese then instantly got in the mood for tacos.

I ran to Dana's room to see if she had a taste for Mexican food as well. I knocked on her door twice, but I didn't get an answer. I peeped in and saw her bed was made and figured she must have left. As I closed her door and headed down the hall, I noticed Sharon's door was cracked. I was going to shut it, but I remembered Sharon always closed her door, so I decided to look inside. As I slowly opened the door, the light from the hall shined across the bed, revealing what seemed to be blood smeared on the sheets. I flung the door open and saw a mess. The room looked like a scene from a movie. The sheets and comforter were ripped. The mirror on the dresser was broken and glass was everywhere. The drawers were opened and the contents were all over the floor. Even Sharon's jewelry box had been shattered.

I ran to the phone to dial 911 then I heard faint sobbing coming from the bathroom in my aunt's room. To my displeasure, there was Dana balled in the fetal position in the bathtub. She had on one of Sharon's lace nightgowns, and it had been torn to shreds. Specks of blood were all over the gown. When she heard me call her name, she turned over to look at me. When I saw her face I began to cry. She looked horrible.

Dana had a swollen left cheek, bloody nose, black eye, and a cut lip. She trembled as she cried. I went to the sink to get her a cold towel to wipe her face then ran to call Sharon at work.

'Sharon, you have to come home quickly. Something horrible has happened to Dana," I said just after she answered the line.

Sharon sounded worried. "What is it? Is she okay?"

"I don't know. She has blood on her, and she's just crying. She won't speak."

"What? I'm on my way. Call the police and stay by her side until I get there," Sharon said as her voice broke.

I hung up the phone and did as Sharon said. Dana sat with tears flooding her face. I took the towel from her and began to clean her face. She cried more and yelled.

"I thought he loved me. How could he do this to me," she cried.

"Who are you talking about, Dana? What happened," I asked, glad to finally hear her talk.

"Travis called and asked could he come over, and I said yes. It was noon, and I knew mom wouldn't come home 'til later. You were at track practice, so I knew I had some time to try to get me some before anyone came home. Well, I wanted it to be special, so I showered in some of mom's perfumed soap and put on one of her gowns. I was going to wash it and return it back to her dresser afterwards, but things didn't go as I had planned.

Travis arrived here about twelve. He was all smiles when he saw me standing in the door looking good. His friends had dropped him off, and he wondered if it was okay if they sat in the car to wait on him. I said it would be fine, but they needed to park in front of another house 'cause we have nosy neighbors. He ran and told them, then returned. We ate sandwiches then went in my room to have sex."

Her tears were still flowing. I felt sorry for her, and I didn't know what to say. She wiped blood from her lip as she continued.

14

"Then the doorbell rang, and I was scared it was one of the neighbors. I made Travis hide in the closet as I put on my robe and went to the door. When I opened the door I was in shock because a guy was standing there. Travis then ran up behind me. He told me he was cool and to let him in.

Dana's nose began to bleed again. I handed her another towel as she went on with the story.

"It was almost one-thirty, and I was getting annoyed with them just hanging out. They were in the kitchen fixing snacks and chilling on the sofa, watching TV. Then his cousin said he had to go to the bathroom. I directed him and returned to the living room. After about five minutes, I began to wonder what he was doing 'cause he hadn't returned.

I found him in my room looking at the pictures stuck on my mirror. I asked if he needed something. He grabbed my arm, pulled me to him, and then kissed me. I forced him into the hall and into the living room, and then told them it was time to leave. He turned to Travis and said, "Man, check your bitch. She tripping and being stingy with the pussy. You better tell her how we roll. Let her know we share the ass."

When Travis laughed, it really pissed me off, and I yelled for them to leave before I called the cops. He then pushed me down to the floor and said, "Bitch, we ain't leaving 'til we get some of this pussy." He ripped the gown, and when I tried to fight back, he hit me several times in the face. The more I screamed and fought back, the harder the hits toward me got. He held my arms while Travis raped me. They switched places and his cousin did the same. I didn't fight them back anymore. All I could do was turn my head away from their faces and cry. As they took turn after turn, I stared at the clock which made me cry even harder. I cried for you, Niyah."

"Why cry for me, Dana," I asked puzzled.

"Because it was five minutes until two. I knew you would be coming home soon. If you came home they would probably rape you, too. I didn't fight back so they would hurry up and leave."

Hearing that brought tears to my eyes. Dana had endured all that pain, thinking of my safety.

She continued, "His cousin hit me one last time in the jaw and dragged me down the hall to my mother's bed and raped me again. While this was going on, Travis rambled through my mother's things. When he got up, I ran for the phone on the nightstand, but he pushed me

15

into the dresser. My head hit the mirror and it shattered. I lay on the floor, playing dead, thinking they'd leave. It worked."

After Dana was done with the story we were both in tears and didn't notice the knocks at the door. The police had arrived. They took pictures and asked plenty of questions. Poor Dana had to endure the horror of telling that story again to them and again when her mother arrived. Sharon was very upset, but supportive. Over the next few weeks, the police had caught all involved. They let Travis go 'cause they didn't have enough evidence on him, but his cousin was arrested because his semen and blood was found on Dana. He got four years for rape, aggravated assault, and petty burglary.

After a month passed, we had begun to put the tragedy behind us, but then we found out Dana was pregnant. She wanted to abort the baby 'cause she knew the pregnancy was a result of the rape. She didn't want a child by Travis's cousin or even him for that matter. But since she was a minor, she couldn't have an abortion without Sharon's permission. Sharon was against abortions, so Dana was forced to go through with the pregnancy.

Dana went into a deep depression. She wouldn't eat for days at a time. One day, I walked in on Dana beating on her stomach in the bathroom. By the summer, when her belly began to bulge out, she threw herself down a flight of stairs, trying to kill the baby.

During all of the turmoil, Sharon and James got back together. He hadn't moved back in, but he was slowly taking over things in the house. Dana and Sharon were already on shaky grounds, and James coming back didn't make it any better.

Toward the middle of August before our tenth grade year, James was ready to move back in. Sharon told Dana that she had been speaking with her father, Martin, and that he said it was okay for her to live with him. When Sharon turned to me, I stormed out and ran to my dresser, and started packing my things.

Dana followed me and sat on the edge of my bed. I stopped packing then sat on the floor with my back to the bed. She rubbed in my hair.

"Why does everything go wrong for me, Dana? My life has been screwed since day one," I said, sulking.

She leaned down and kissed the top of my head. "Don't worry, Niyah. We still have each other," she said.

I smiled. She continued to console me.

"Don't worry. You'll like living with my dad. Mom said he has three bedrooms. I'm sure he won't mind us both coming to live with him."

I had begun to get happy again. Just then Sharon came into the room and interrupted us. "Niyah, you didn't even let me finish," she said.

"What is there to add, Sharon? I know the routine by now."

Sharon sat on the bed next to Dana. "You haven't even heard if you have to leave, and you're in here packing."

"Whenever I get happy and comfortable with where I am, it's time to move again. It's seems as if one year is all people can tolerate with me,' I responded.

Sharon began to cry. "Sweetie, it just didn't work out the way I planned. James and I are happy, and we're starting our lives over."

Right before Labor Day weekend, Dana and I were all packed and off to Martin's place. When we pulled up to his home, it reminded me of a chapel. He came out with a broad smile on his face. I hadn't seen him in years, but he still looked the same. He was six-feet-tall with a medium build and was very dark skinned. His skin looked smooth and creamy like chocolate milk. He dressed professionally, and he wore a lot of cologne. He helped clear Dana's things out of the trunk.

"Niyah, give your cousin a hug so we can go," Sharon said.

"Go where? Dana and I thought I was staying here too," I asked.

"No, I told Martin I wouldn't do that to him, even though he said it was okay."

"You didn't tell me. Where will I be staying then," I asked, yelling.

"I spoke with your aunt, Lena, and she wants you to stay with her."

I slowly walked over and hugged Dana.

"I'll miss you," Dana said.

"I'll miss you too," I replied.

Martin came up to me. He hugged and kissed me on my forehead and handed me a small piece of paper.

"This is the phone number and address so you girls can keep in touch," he said.

"Thanks, Martin," I said as I took the paper.

I turned and walked back to the car and cried all the way to Lena's house. I thought to myself, *why do grown-ups always ruin their children's lives*? Here I am fourteen and have lived in three different places. Not just because of moving to new environments, but new families as well.

I thought about all the different homes I'd been in and then I thought about my father. He moved to California with a white woman. Grandma Ella told me he was back in town, and looking for me, but I always wondered why he never tried to locate me before. Being an only child, I never really had anyone, but Dana or my friends to be there for me. Whenever I moved, I tried not to make new friends. Dating guys was an awful ordeal, too. I'd meet a guy; get to know him, then have to move away, never to hear from them again.

Demonte and I was getting to know each other on a different level. We had sex for the first time, and then we were expressing how we felt about each other. I held the small heart pendant in my hand and thought about when I had to tell him I was moving away.

We sat on top of his father's truck, watching the stars. I told him about Dana's ordeal since that was the reason he and I hadn't talked to each other. He was truly hurt, and I came to realize he actually cared for me. It was getting late, and I was going to be in trouble for being out late, so I jumped down off the truck to leave. As I bent to get my purse and shoes, Demonte grabbed me. He swung me around and kissed me passionately.

"Call me as soon as you get to wherever you'll be staying," he said.

"I will," I responded sadly.

"Niyah, I don't want our relationship to end over a move."

I sat there speechless. The situation took me for a loop 'cause in the past I'd always break things off so I would have no baggage left behind to remember. But breaking up was hard to do with Demonte 'cause he was always on my mind.

# SECTION 2

Troubled Times

Chapter 3


    As we turned into the driveway, I looked at the small house then thought to myself, *I wonder how long I'll be able to call this place home.* The whole atmosphere was different. It was a bad neighborhood. There were run down cars sitting on bricks, stray dogs, and cats running through all the yards, and tons of little kids playing in the middle of the street. I was almost afraid to get out of the car. My aunt, Lena, came out of the house looking a hot mess from head to toe. I stood, trying my best to figure out when hot pink and lime green start matching together in fashion. And her red sandals just topped off the whole outfit. She ran and hugged aunt Sharon then turned to comment on how much I had grown up. She rejoiced on how much I looked like, my mother, Rosa. I gave her a fake smile and hug.

    I grabbed my suitcases and duffel bags out of the trunk. Lena's husband and two of his friends were sitting on the porch laughing and drinking beer. They didn't even flinch when I struggled with all the bags. I thought to myself, *you fat bastards. You could at least help me.* Just as I dropped two of my bags, a young male, who had been eyeing me from across the street, ran over to help me. His friends made remarks about how he was trying to show off for the new chic on the block. He paid them no mind. He introduced himself then grabbed most of my bags.

    "Hello, Antonio. My name is Niyah. Thanks for helping out with my bags," I said.

    As we walked up the oil stained driveway, we passed two broken down, tireless cars, I noticed there was no grass in the yard, only dirt. Sharon came up behind me, kissed me on the cheek, and quickly ran off to her car. I stood there broken hearted as she drove off. If Antonio hadn't been there, I would have cried. After a few seconds,

I turned to find Antonio grinning from ear to ear. I smiled back as we walked on into the house. I wondered if Antonio thought I owed him something for helping me.

The house was small but it was home, and I was going to make the best of it. My room was at the end of the hall. It was much smaller than the one at Sharon's house. Lena hadn't cleaned or gotten the room ready for me at all. It was cluttered and, the floor looked as if it hadn't been vacuumed in days. I couldn't see the bed because there was a massive pile of clothes on it. I dropped my things on the floor then scanned over everything.

"Damn baby girl you got a task ahead of you," Antonio said as he entered the room.

I pushed back some clothes, plopped down on the bed, and put my hands up to my eyes. I cried like a baby. Antonio sat down next to me and rubbed my back. I leaned on his shoulder. I told him the whole story of my life. He listened with much concern.

"Well thank you for helping me. You can go back to your friends. I need to try to clean this place up," I said.

Lena came in and spoke to him.

"How is your brother doing Antonio," she asked him.

"He's ok," he replied.

"Niyah, you hungry," she finally asked me.

"No. I'm okay for now."

"We're stepping out for a bit, and won't be back until later. Here's twenty dollars incase you want to eat something. Maybe you and Antonio can order a pizza.

"Yeah that sounds cool," Antonio answered for me.

"Thanks for the money Lena, but Antonio is on his way out behind you," I said.

She turned to walk away then shortly came back.

"While it's on my mind, let me tell you the rules of the house. You only have three rules to abide by here, young lady. Go to school everyday that you're suppose to go. Don't bother anything that doesn't belong to you. And no getting pregnant while living here. I can't really give you curfew, because I'm rarely here.

"I don't have a car or a driver's license, so I won't be out late anyway," I responded.

"Okay then. Also, if you get in trouble with the law, don't call me to help you out."

A few minutes after Lena left out of room I heard what sounded like a rocket crank up. I watched as they drove off in a very old truck.

"I'm about to change into some cleaning clothes so do you mind stepping out," I asked Antonio.

"You ain't got nothing I ain't already seen. And call me Tone, all my friends do," he said with a smirk on his face.

"Okay Tone."

I undressed as he watched me out of the side of his eyes. I put on my track shorts and a tank top. I dusted all the furniture in the room while Tone vacuumed. We both folded all the clothes then put them into a large box. Tone took the box to Lena's room, and then helped me make up the bed. I had brought my lavender comforter set from Sharon's, along with the ballerina pictures. I hung my ballerina pictures to accent the room. It only took about an hour to actually clean the room.

"I'm going to take a shower. I'd really appreciate what you've done but you can leave now," I said to Tone.

"I really enjoyed talking and spending time with you. Let's order that pizza Lena was talking about," he said.

"I guess I owe you some food for all the help you've given me. I'll order it after my shower," I said.

I got my shower caddy basket then went into the bathroom. I tied my hair up into a bun.

I had a little trick up my sleeve.

*How far is this boy willing to go to impress me,* I pondered.

After brushing my teeth and washing my face, I went back to my room. Tone was sitting patiently awaiting my return.

"Would you like to join me," I said jokingly.

"Yes," he replied to my surprise.

I'd never seen a boy undress so fast. We had sex in the shower with the water steaming up the mirrors.

After we got dressed, I ordered the pizza. I let him brush and play in my hair until the delivery guy came. We lounged on the couch, as we ate and watched cartoons. We cleaned up our little mess, and then returned to my room. As we sat on the bed, Tone played with my toes.

"Where do you see yourself in five years," he asked me.

"Once I finish high school and college I want to become a famous author. Maybe get married and have a few kids. What about you?"

"After I go to college I plan on being drafted into the NFL. I don't know about marriage, but I do want a son."

I felt so comfortable talking with him.

"Did your boyfriend give you that necklace," he asked pointing at my neck.

"Yeah, but we aren't together anymore," I said lying.

"Why you still wearing it if he's your ex?"

"We broke up because I had to move away. I don't want to talk about it," I said as I turned my back to him to lie down.

"It's getting late. Do you need to go home and check in," I asked him.

"No. I live with my older brother, but he's never home."

"Where are your parents," I asked concerned.

"Both of my parents were killed in a bad car wreck when I was younger, and my older brother, Michael, has been taking care of me."

I felt so sad. Although I didn't live with either one, at least I still had both of my parents. I guess everyone goes through trials and tribulations in their life.

I use to get so wrapped up in my problems I never realized other people go through things almost just as bad.

"You sleepy?"

"A little," I said after a yawn.

"Do you mind if I stay for a little while longer," he asked.

I moved closer to him and he wrapped his arms around me, as I pulled the covers over us. The room was completely dark, and the only thing that could be heard was the humming of my fan. Tone kissed the back of my neck then wrapped his arms around my stomach, holding me tightly. He quickly fell asleep snoring. The last thing I remembered hearing was that loud truck pulling in the driveway and the headlights dancing across the walls.

The next morning I awoke to Tone's face.

*Damn I didn't expect him to actually spend the night,* I thought to myself.

I slowly removed his arm then walked down the hall to the bathroom. I figured everyone was sleep because the house was so quiet. I stood there staring at my reflection in the mirror. I contemplated a nice way to tell Tone to leave. He'd already overstayed his welcome. I returned to the room and found him sitting on the edge of the bed, getting dressed.

"I didn't intend to stay so late. My bad," he said.

I was so relieved that I didn't have to say anything. I put my robe on and walked him to the door. We stood there in silence a few minutes as if we were trying to find the right words to say.

"I really enjoyed spending time with you Niyah. Do you think it would be possible to do it again?"

"What," I asked puzzled.

"Not the sex part, but the hanging out part," he corrected.

I frowned at him.

"I mean. . . look the sex was wonderful, and I wouldn't mind doing that again, but I enjoyed talking to you more." He paused then continued.

"I have a girlfriend, and she's cool, but we can't talk like you and I can. She is so serious all the time."

"Tone, you're cool company, and I really enjoyed hanging together. I'm not looking for a boyfriend. I'm a loner, and I like it that way. See, this way nobody gets hurt, but we can see where things go," I said.

He kissed me on my cheek.

"I understand, and I won't push myself on you."

"Good 'cause I don't like it when people crowd me out. I like my space," I said.

"Niyah I get what you are saying, but I'm really digging you."

I just starred at him. He turned the doorknob and opened the door, and slowly walked out.

He made it halfway down the driveway when I ran in the house to jot down my phone number on a piece of paper. I ran out and gave it to him. He looked at it.

"I thought you said you didn't want me crowding you."

"It's just a number, boy, not the keys to the house. Now do me a favor and keep what happened between us a secret.

"I will," he promised.

I closed my robe because I felt a chill draft. He pecked me on my forehead and turned to walk away. I went to my room and peeped out of my blinds and watched him jog to his house.

# CHAPTER 4

I threw myself down on the bed, starring at the ceiling wondering if I should call Demonte. I honestly cared about him, and I knew how he felt about me, but I didn't want to hurt his feelings. I looked over at the clock. It was almost noon. I'd never slept that late before. I picked up the phone and dialed Demonte's number.

"Hello," a female voice said.

I hung up. I slowly pressed the buttons, and the girl answered again.

"Yeah," she said with a slight attitude.

"May I speak to Demonte," I finally asked.

"Hold on," she said.

I could hear her telling Demonte that he had a phone call. It wasn't until she giggled that I realized who she was. It was Rashonda, his ex-girlfriend. She was on the cheerleading squad at Havenview. He claimed she cheated on him, and he couldn't stand her.

"What number shows up on the caller ID box," he asked Rashonda.

"It says Lena Dodges," she replied.

"That's my cousin, I've been awaiting her call," he said lying.

When he said hello on the phone I hung up in his face. We hadn't said we had broken up, but I guess he had moved on. Demonte called back twice, but I ignored each call. There's no need in crying over spilled milk now. It was time for me to do the same, and get on with my life. I jumped up to make the best of my Saturday. I ate a bowl of cereal then showered. I put on my white and yellow sports bra and matching track shorts. I sprayed some baby powder perfume over my body, put my hair in a ponytail, and slipped on my running shoes. I checked myself in the mirror one more time. I could pass for eighteen, and that was with no makeup. I warmed up at the gate by the carport door. After a few stretches I was ready to run. As I rounded my side of the block, I saw Tone and a few friends putting up a basketball goal in the middle of the street. I stopped in front of my house. After a few moments of rest I started back running.

"Sweetness, come here for a minute," Tone called out to me from down the street.

As I walked up his driveway he came down to meet me.

Soon Tone's buddies grouped around us. Tone introduced them to me.

"Oh, so we finally meet the person that hogged all my boy's time from us yesterday," the fat one said.

"Whatever. Tone could have left when he wanted to. There was no gun to his head," I replied.

The other guys laughed.

"Sexy, and sassy, just the way I like them," Tone said with that cute smile.

I began to sweat from the sun's heat.

"You want something to drink," Tone asked me. "You seem hot."

"Sure. Thanks," I replied.

"Come on in. You can meet Michael, my brother."

I followed Tone into the kitchen. The house was similar to Lena's house on the outside, but it was a typical male house. It had leather furniture and naked African art everywhere. Michael was sitting on the couch playing a Nintendo game.

"Make sure that door is closed all the way so you won't be letting the air out," he shouted.

"Yo, bro'. This is Niyah, the girl I told you about," Tone said.

"So you the reason my brother didn't come home last night," Michael asked me.

"Yeah, but it was his choice," I responded.

"The right choice, I say. My name is Michael, but you can call me Mike," he said reaching to shake my hand.

"Nice to meet you. My name is Niyah."

Tone handed me a glass of apple juice, then went back out the door and asked me to meet him out there whenever I was done. Mike starred while I drank.

"So y'all live here alone," I asked, breaking the silence.

"Yeah, we do," he replied."

"How old are you," I asked.

"Twenty-three."

"May I ask your age as well?"

"I'll be fifteen in December," I bragged.

"You a runner," he asked pointing at my clothes.

"I use to be at my old school."

I smiled when I caught him checking me out on the slick side.

"You trying to get information to share with your brother?"

"Something like that," he said with a grin plastered on his face.

"Don't waste your time, 'cause your brother and I are just friends and nothing else. Besides he has a girlfriend."

"Who? Tawanda, the duck?"

He walked over to the TV and picked up a picture. I looked at the portrait of her and laughed. She resembled a bird by the mouth a little. I handed him back the photo and he rubbed my hand

"Just friends you say?"

"Yes," I stated again.

"Cool. Maybe we can be friends too."

"Who knows?"

"Don't be a stranger Niyah," Mike said, as he held the door open for me to walk out.

Tone took off his shirt and ran up to me and wrapped his arms around my waist.

"What took you so long," he asked.

"Oh! I was just looking at pictures of your girlfriend."

All of his friends laughed and made quacking sounds.

"I'm going to kill Mike," he said angrily.

"It isn't his fault you're dating a duck," I said laughing.

"Whatever," he said angrily.

I could tell Tone wasn't in a joking mood, so I went home.

I took a long warm bath, then sat on my bed and wrote in my journal. I liked Tone but I didn't want to rush into anything 'cause he already had a girl. I couldn't quite tell what Tone wanted from me, but I knew Mike just wanted some ass from the way he flirted with me. But I wasn't even going to get involved with him like that.

I found out Sharon had Lena register me in school already. My thought on that was that she had it planned out a while that I'd be living here.

That Monday morning, Tone and I walked to school. In a few months, I would be fifteen, and I was in the tenth grade. I was going to make the best out of it for sure. It took us about ten minutes to get to school 'cause we kept goofing off on the way.

The school was much bigger than my previous school. As we struggled through the crowded hallway, a girl grabbed his arm. She was happy to see him and was grinning while she hugged him. I recognized her from the photo. It was Tawanda.

"And you are," Tawanda asked smiling.

"I'm Niyah. I'm new to this school."

"Cool. Girl, you'll like it here. I see my boyfriend is being a gentleman and showing you around."

"Yes, he's quite the charmer," I said giving her the fakest smile I could muster.

"We live on the same street. He helped me with my bags when I moved in this past weekend. I also met his brother Mike."

"How nice. We've been dating for a year and I haven't seen his house yet," she said with a slight attitude.

"What a shame. It's such a nice home. You should ask to come over some time," I said, adding salt to the wound.

"I'll have to do so," she replied.

I could tell I wasn't going to like her much. She wore her hair in a tree ponytail style, and her complexion was black as tar. I wanted to tell her that her hairdo drew too much attention to her big, duck bill lips. I had to give it to her. She was a nice dresser, but she was a little on the chunky side. She kept giving me funny looks as we walked down the hall. I wanted to know what her deal was. I mean damn. I had on some black jean shorts and a black and purple-stripped tank top. Hell, I couldn't help it if my clothes fit me just right.

We stopped in front of a set of lockers. Tone told me I could share the locker with him and gave me the combination. I put up my belongings as she whined about how he never shared one with her. His reply was she never asked. He introduced me to a few guys that were standing around. They were all on the football team with Tone.

"Do you play any sports because your legs are so muscular," Aaron asked.

"I use to run track and play volleyball at my old school," I replied.

"Yeah, I talked her into trying out for our track team. We could use the speed," Tone said.

"How do you know she got speed," Tawanda asked.

"I watched her run around the block this past weekend. She has form and stamina," Tone said.

All of us broke out into laughter except for Tawanda who was now giving me the mean eye.

"Isn't your last name Smith," Tone asked me.

"Yes," I replied.

"My last name is Sutton. I think we are in the same homeroom class," he said with his hand extended.

Tone grabbed my hand and rushed me off to class. Tawanda stopped him to hug and kiss him. The whole time he was still holding my hand. She saw he was still holding onto my arm and gave me a dirty look. If she only knew I did more than hold hands the other night.

"Meet me at the lockers at lunchtime," Tawanda said to Tone.

"Okay," Tone said as we walked off to class.

Tone and I had three classes other than homeroom together. I liked him walking me around, but he was beginning to cramp my style. Guys wouldn't want to talk to me with him stuck to my side. When the lunch bell rang, we put up our things and walked on to the cafeteria.

"Aren't you gonna wait on your woman," I asked Tone sarcastically.

"She knows where the cafeteria is," he replied smugly.

We went through the line and got our food and were all seated when she met up with us.

"You bastard! Why didn't you wait on me," Tawanda asked pointing in Tone's face.

He was trying to calm her down when I stood up.

"Look, Tone. Believe me, I love the attention you have showed me since we first met, and you have helped me so much, but this drama is giving me a headache. I'll catch up to you later."

He grabbed my tray and begged me to sit down, but he soon turned his attention back to the loud drama queen. I went over to eat lunch with Sandra, a cool girl I met in English class. After school I met Tone at the locker.

"Do you want me to escort you home," he asked as he put his books away.

"No. I'm going to track try-outs this afternoon."

"Well, I'll tag along so I can walk you home afterwards. Can't have a fine ass shorty like you going home by yourself in the dark. You need a strong man to protect you."

"I can handle my own and you know this," I said as I playfully punched him in the arm.

"You sure can," he said staring into my eyes.

"But you can wait on me," I said as I closed the locker.

The hall was empty.

"I missed you so much today, and couldn't wait to feel those juicy ass lips."

He then started licking his as we leaned in for a kiss.

"Tone! Tone," Tawanda yelled from down the hall just as we were about to embrace.

We both walked toward her as she shot me another ugly look.

"I need to talk to you, now," Tawanda said to Tone.

"Can it wait 'til later?"

"Uh, 'cuse me. No it can't," Tawanda retorted.

"I just want to know why you been acting funny lately."

"I got a lot on my mind. I'm sorry if you felt that way," Tone said to her.

"Excuse me, but Tone I have tryouts to attend. I'll see you later," I said as I turned to leave.

I don't know what else was said, but when I looked back they were embracing.

Only about ten girls tried out. The coach clearly stated she only needed three good runners. Our speed, stance, endurance, and ability to jump hurdles in a timely manner were tested. After about an hour and a half trials were over, Coach congratulated us all and said the list with the three names would be up the next afternoon in front of the gym. As I went and collected my things, I saw Tone waiting, on the bleachers.

"You looked good out there. Like running is something you really love," he said.

I just rolled my eyes and continued packing my things.

"Running is a passion of mines," I finally replied.

"Excuse me Niyah Smith. Have you ever ran before," the Coach asked me.

"At my old school," I replied.

"I could tell by your breathing and warming up techniques. You had a good try-out," she said shaking my hand.

"Thanks, but it really wasn't my best."

"You still looked better than some of the girls already on the team," she said smiling.

Tone and I left out of the gym, and started our long walk home.

"You wanna race," he asked.

"Yeah, why not," I replied as I took off running.

When he finally caught up to me, he pushed me in the back.

"You cheater! You left before I said go."

"Man, please. You just got dusted. Admit it."

I went in and got settled for bed. Tone called me later that night and we fell asleep on the phone. Tone was really beginning to make me ponder on being more than friends with him.

CHAPTER 5

The next six weeks was a breeze. Tone and I walked to and from school, and since I had made the track team, Mike, his brother, would pick us up in the afternoon. Yeah, everything was going wonderful. Right. Wonderful, but I was crying and scared shitless as I sat in my friend Sandra's bathroom awaiting the results of my pregnancy test? Sandra and I had become real close friends. We both stood there shocked as the result window turned pink, a positive indication I was pregnant.

"What are you going to do girl," Sandra asked.

"I can't have this baby. I'm fourteen. I'll get put out of my house if my aunt finds out," I said with my head down.

"You going to tell Tone?"

"Absolutely not. I told Tone I was on my cycle, so he doesn't know anything. And I plan to keep it that way. I don't need that extra drama right now.

"Abort it then," she said holding my hand.

"Would you go with me to get it done," I asked her sadly.

"Sure. My sister Keisha works at the abortion clinic."

That night I talked to Keisha on the phone and let her in on everything. She told me that I was a minor and couldn't get it done without my parents or guardians' permission, but she would take care of that part for me since she knew me. That Thursday we went to the clinic. We cut school and caught the bus. I had my checkup for further proof of pregnancy. I was six weeks pregnant give or take a few days.

"You sure about this," Keisha asked.

"Yes," I said with a bowed head.

Sandra and I waited in the lobby for my name to be called. I noticed all of the women sitting with their heads down, waiting for their names to be called as well. Shame is what I guess they felt 'cause it seemed like grief sat on their shoulders, with all the down faces. I wasn't sad, but relieved that I had a way to have a second chance at life.

"Niyah Smith," the receptionist called from the desk.

I walked over to her.

"Yes mam. I'm Niyah."

"Right this way dear. The doctor is ready to see you."

I followed her into a room.

"Change into this robe. The nurse will be in to prep you," she said before leaving."

Keisha came in and hugged me.

"How are you feeling," she asked me.

"I'm fine."

"Well, let's get started."

She opened the folder and paperwork they had me fill out previously in the lobby about my health background. She pulled out a pen and signed in the place of the guardian. I had her sign my mother's name just in case any problems arose.

She handed me a small cup of water and a pill and wrote some more information in my chart.

"Now that pill will stop the heartbeat of the fetus. So make sure you are actually ready to proceed," she said looking directly at me.

I knew that there would be no turning back once I took it. I drank the water and swallowed the pill.

"Okay, now lie on the examining bed and wait for about 30 minutes."

I sat there staring at the ceiling thinking about what I'd just done to my baby. Physically I couldn't feel any pain, but my heart sobbed for the life growing inside of me. Just as a tear fell the doctor walked in.

"Ms. Smith. I see you have been prepped. Do you understand the steps of the procedure ahead of you," he asked adjusting his glasses.

"No. I don't."

"First I'll check to see if the pill did its job of deadening the embryo. Once that is confirmed, I will insert this suture tube and remove the fetus and sac matter. Then you will be cleaned and directed to our observation room, where you can rest until you are fully recovered."

The doctor was really nice and polite on informing me. I was a little nervous, but I knew it had to be done. The whole procedure took about thirty minutes. I felt a little sad afterwards, but it was for the best.

On Friday I cut school again and stayed over Sandra's house. I gave Tone an excuse about bad cramps. Saturday and Sunday I just lounged around the house.

Monday morning, as Tone and I walked to school, he held my hand and kissed my cheek. He gave me so many mixed signals. He was still with Tawanda. I thought to myself about our child and what he/she would have looked like or been like. Something in the back of my mind said to tell him, but I wasn't going to. What he didn't know wouldn't hurt him.

After two weeks things were starting to get back to normal. November 4th was volleyball try-outs. I had been looking forward to those for days. At three o'clock some more girls and I were waiting in the gym for Coach Tulison. She was a mean and stern coach, but that was cool with me, 'cause sometimes I needed the extra push to put forth my all.

To my displeasure, Tawanda was the captain of the team. She had the biggest grin on her face when she saw me trying out. Tone wanted to wait on me during practice, but I turned him down. He was so protective of me walking home late in the evenings. I was glad I sent him home 'cause Tawanda was already in a bitchy mood, and seeing him there waiting on me wouldn't have made it any better. They were still dating, but she didn't understand the type of friendship Tone and I shared.

Coach stated that she would let Tawanda lead us through the try-outs. Tawanda started out teaching warm-up and cool down techniques. Then she taught us how to serve, hit, and punt the ball. In order to see how fit we were, we had to do arm, and leg exercises, and then run in place. Tawanda yelled that we couldn't stop 'til she told us to. Some people weren't able to keep up. After a while all the other girls had stopped, but I was still running. Tawanda hadn't blown the whistle, and I wasn't about to let her see me give up. She walked right up to me and just stood there, grinning.

"Had enough," Tawanda asked as she glared at me.

"Not until you blow the whistle," I said calmly.

"Well, you're the one running, not me, so we'll see who'll get tired first," she said.

After a few minutes, some of the girls on the team were telling her that it was enough and to let me stop. She didn't say anything but stare at me as if she was trying to locate the coward in me.

"Sure you aren't getting tired," Tawanda asked me again.

I looked right into her chubby face.

"Sweetie, you fail to realize I'm on the track team. I'm the best 200-meter runner on the team. I have to run more than this in practice. So bring it on," I said sarcastically.

I was sweaty, and my legs were throbbing, but I guess me not wanting to giving up is what motivated me to drive on further. Tawanda then blew the whistle 'cause she knew she'd lost the battle. She set us up for a game.

Shockingly, she picked me to be on her team. The test was to calculate our ball handling and eye coordinating skills. I stood by the net as she served. The ball hit me in the back of the head. I turned around in pain.

"I'm so sorry. It was truly an accident," Tawanda said.

Deep down I knew she did it on purpose. When it happened again, Tawanda decided I should move to a different floor position. When I went up to spike a ball, Tawanda ran into my side on the way down. I hit the floor hard. I had to lay there for a while. Coach Tulison came to see if I was okay and helped me up.

"Tawanda, calm down your roughness a little," Coach Tulison said.

Tawanda just stood smiling and grinning.

"If Niyah can't deal with toughness, then maybe she should go tryout for the cheerleading squad or something," she said looking in my direction.

"I'm alright. I can play. Let me serve the ball this time," I said as I got up.

Tawanda threw it at my face full force, but I caught it before it could hit me. She had crossed the line, and I was ready to wipe that grin off her face.

Coach Tulison blew the whistle to end try-outs. Tawanda and a few of her friends turned and walked toward the bleachers. I ran up behind Tawanda and pushed her, face first, into the stands. When she finally got up, I sucker punched her in the left jaw. The fight was on. We were scratching and pulling each other's hair. I took someone's English book and slapped her across the face with it. But, I won't lie Tawanda got some good licks in on me.

"Resolve this on your own time and not on my court," Coach Tulison demanded.

We weren't bleeding, but we were both sweating and breathing hard. I gathered my things and walked towards the door.

"Bitch, stay away from my man. He don't want yo' skank ass," Tawanda yelled.

"Hoe, you blind? It isn't me who is on him. He's on me. He calls and walks with me to class and from school and even to each of my classes during the day. Hell, he even holds my hand in front of you. I share a locker and have been to his house before you. But you're his so-called girlfriend. Please don't waste your words on me. Tell your so-called man. Oh yeah and if you should call tonight and the line is busy, then it would be me telling him how I whipped your sorry ass today," I said.

I could tell she was mad by the look on her face.

It was dark when I stepped outside. Tawanda and her friends came out the side door and were mumbling to themselves as they walked toward me. I put on my backpack and readied myself for the long walk home. I was waiting for her ass to do or say something. The mood I was in, I could have killed or hurt any one of them. Just then Mike, Tone's brother, pulled up.

"Tone told me you'd be getting out of try-outs late, and to come and pick you up. Y'all must be really close friends huh," he asked.

I didn't give a reply. He got out opening the door for me. I put my things in the backseat. I was so happy because I was sore from head to toe. My legs felt like spaghetti noodles.

"What is up with yo' hair? You been in a fight or something," he asked as he got back in the driver's seat.

"Actually I was," I replied.

I recapped the whole squabble to him.

"I'm glad you whopped her ass, 'cause I never liked her. She always gets an attitude if she calls and Tone isn't there, or I'm on the other line," he said smiling.

41

We both laughed as he pulled off.

The smooth ride lulled me to sleep.

"Hey sleepy head," Mike said, as he rubbed the side of my face.

We pulled up in his driveway and he helped me out of the car. When I got out I noticed the curtains in the kitchen moved.

"Thank you for picking me up," I said.

"No problem cutie."

Just as I began to walk towards my house, Tone ran out and caught up with me.

"Tawanda called and told me what happened today. How could you jump on her like that," he asked yelling at me.

She'd totally twisted the story around and said I beat her up 'cause I was mad that Tone was with her and not me.

"I ain't got time for this. You're gonna believe her lies anyway so what's the use," I said getting a little agitated.

"I told you I didn't want any conflicts," he said.

"She's the one that came at me with the drama. It's late. I'm going home," I said leaving him standing on the curb.

I couldn't believe he was upset with me. He wasn't even trying to hear my side at all.

*I knew no good would come out of this situation,* I thought to myself.

The following morning, as I entered the main hall of the school, Tone walked right past me. He hadn't spoken a word to me since I left him standing in the street the other night. As I headed toward his locker with Sandra, I noticed a small group standing there. And heard Tawanda talking.

"You're with me and it's time you acted like it," she said to Tone.

I still couldn't see because there were people in the way. When the people dispersed I saw Tawanda had pulled my things out of the locker and onto the floor. Tone looked up and saw me, then walked away. I was so pissed. I could have slapped the black off that girl, but Sandra beat me to it. Sandra and Tawanda were rolling on the ground on my things. Sandra was short and skinny, but home girl could fight. I pulled her up before she got in trouble. Sandra was mad at me 'cause I didn't jump in.

"Why didn't you help," she asked.

"Some people are ignorant and thrive off of stupid things. You can't stoop to Tawanda's level," I replied. "I'll take you up on sharing your locker."

"Okay, Sandra said helping me gather my books.

Tawanda and her friends called us bitches as they walked past us and I had to contain Sandra again.

After lunch, we returned to our locker to see Tawanda and two of her girls running away. 'Two Bitches Here', was written in big black letters over the door. I pulled out my black marker from math class and added a couple of words. It now read 'The two bitches here rule'. Sandra and I high-fived and laughed as we went our separate ways to class.

For the next few weeks, I steered clear of Tone.

CHAPTER 6

I woke up and realized I was late for school. I quickly showered and dressed and rushed off. I went into the attendance office to sign in for being tardy. As I walked back out I noticed Tone crying in the corner.

I didn't know what to think. I went over to him and bent down on my knees so we could be eye-to-eye. I rubbed his knee and wiped his tears away with a Kleenex from my purse. He was shaking and trembling. I'd never seen him like this and it was beginning to scare me.

"I can't believe it," he mumbled.

"What is it Tone," I asked.

"What am I going to do now," he shouted.

"Just tell me, what it is," I said anxiously.

"Mike was in a bad wreck. He fell asleep behind the wheel and ran head on into a semi-truck. He was thrown through the windshield and died on contact," he said sadly.

I couldn't breath, and it felt like my heart skipped a beat. I waited for him to say it was a joke, but that never happened. My knees went limp and I sat on to the floor.

"I can't believe he's gone. He dropped me off this morning," Tone said.

I held his hand and leaned my head on his shoulder. I felt his pain. He had lost everything, even both his parents and brother to horrible car wrecks.

That afternoon he came home with me. We sat on my bed in silence as he laid his head in my lap.

The next couple of days dragged on. Tone had brought over some clothes and slept on our couch. After the funeral, he continued to stay with us. Marty, his uncle, was in Germany in the Army. He was coming to live in Mike and Tone's house to take care of Tone, but it would take ten weeks before he could get back to the states. Lena confirmed it was okay for Tone to stay with us 'til Marty got there.

After two weeks, things finally started falling back into place. Tone and I were talking and laughing again.

One particular night, I awoke from a bad dream. I was sweating so I took off my robe. I lay in bed and listened to the raindrops splash against my window. I opened my eyes and watched shadows of the rain on the ceiling. They trickled down the window seal like tears on a face. I looked at the clock and it read eleven. I heard Lena telling Tone she was gone and to lock the door behind her. It was the weekend. She and the girls from work always went to the casino on Saturdays. I lay there for about twenty minutes, trying to fall back asleep. It wasn't working, so I went to the bathroom and washed my face with a warm towel then went in the kitchen and heated up some left over roast beef and vegetables.

I saw the TV light go off in the living room and guessed Tone was going to sleep. When I peeked in, I saw him lying on his back with his arms folded behind his head. He was starring at the ceiling. I told him good night and turned to walk away when he called me to come to him. I came in and stood near the couch.

Tone reached for my hand and pulled me near him. He ran his hand up the back of my thighs under my nightshirt and up my leg. I swiftly pushed his hand away. He gave me an intoxicating glare with his big brown eyes.

"Goodnight, Tone," I said as I left the room.

"Don't leave me alone," he said reaching for me.

I went into the hall closet to retrieve a pillow and blanket then went back in the living room. I climbed up on the ledge of the picture window. After what seemed like a long time, I finally fell asleep.

I felt the covers move and woke to see Tone with a pillow in his hand standing near me. Something told me to make him go back to the couch, but I let him climb up with me. I made him go to the other end. We propped our pillows up, and I put my feet in his lap.

He broke the silence between us.

"I know we've been through a lot, but I want you to know that I love you."

Those words really took me by surprise, 'cause he's never told me how he felt.

"I can no longer hide my true feelings for you. Life is too short. I know Tawanda and I are together, but I promise you from the bottom of my heart that I will leave her and love only you if you say you want to be with me. Please tell me you feel the same way 'cause I can't stand to lose you again."

I didn't say anything. I looked out the window the whole time he talked. I had a feeling he was saying those things just to get into my panties. I turned to him to tell him where to get off with all those lies, but he was crying again. Not just a few tears, but streams falling down his cheeks. I felt sorry for him 'cause I hadn't seen him cry like that since Mike died. I used one end of the blanket to wipe his face. I held his arm and caressed his face to let him know everything would be okay.

"Tone, I do love you. I have since I first met you. You are different from any guy I've known, and I will always cherish that. But you broke my heart by choosing to continue to stay with Tawanda even after what we shared. Let's take things slow and see how they go," I said.

A slight smile inched across his face. I smiled back as he opened his arms for a hug. I tried to oblige, but he wanted me closer. He grabbed my legs and pulled me to him. He was sitting Indian-style, and I sat on top of his lap with my legs around his waist. There we sat, locked in an embrace. I could feel his penis swelling up through his boxers, and it was turning me on in a big way. He leaned in to kiss me, and I let him. I had really missed his lips. His tongue explored my mouth like he was searching for buried treasure. I pulled his shirt over his head and rubbed my fingers across his chest and down his stomach across his muscles. After we made love we fell asleep in each other's arms.

For eight weeks we were in love. He did just as he promised and broke up with Tawanda. He was finally my man, and I was his woman, I felt there wasn't a human on earth that could change that.

Tone was my best friend as well as my lover. Who would have known we would be back like this?

School was over, and Tone was working in a video store. He claimed he was saving up to by a car, 'cause he had gotten his learner's permit once he turned sixteen. I was a young woman now, and I had grown so much over the years. I had a man I loved dearly, and I was closer to my mother and grandmother more than ever before. When school started, we would be in the eleventh grade. Tone told me he wanted to go to a local University, and play football. I always wanted to be a writer, so I was going to major in journalism and literature. I had folders of poems and short stories saved to one day get published. Tone use to always joke with me and saying I could be the next Terry McMillan.

We agreed to finish college then get married. He would always say when he entered the NFL he would move us away and buy a huge house for us to raise our children. That upcoming weekend, his uncle Marty was due back to America. Lena and I went to Mike's house and cleaned it up since nobody had lived there since the funeral. We had a barbecue for his uncle when he came home to show appreciation for fighting for his country.

Marty was so happy to see Tone 'cause he hadn't seen him in years. Tone moved back home and it was okay with me as long as our time together didn't change. I would go and spend the night there sometimes. Things seemed nice at first.

It was now the middle of August. Tone and I had saved up a bit of money. He had already gone to a couple of places to look at cars. Marty made a big dinner and invited Lena and me over to their house. He said he had a big announcement to make to all of us. After dinner he stood and said that he and Tone would be moving to Germany. Tone nearly choked on his drink. The room was so silent you could hear a pin drop to the floor. Marty said he had married a German girl, and because of her country's rules, she couldn't leave to come to America. Since Tone was a minor, he would have to go back to Germany with him. Tone seemed more shocked than me. I knew things were too good to be true. I burst out in tears, and ran back to the house and locked myself in my room.

# SECTION 3

## The Big Move

Chapter 7

In two days I would be saying goodbye to the one I loved. I figured I'd never see him again. I had avoided Tone for a week. I wouldn't answer the phone or return his calls. If he left messages I'd erase them without listening to them. I didn't want any baggage or memory of him when he left.

The night before his flight to Germany, I went and spent the night over Sandra's house so I wouldn't see him. It was tearing me up inside, but I felt staying away from him was the best way to get over Tone.

The next afternoon I returned home. Lena told me Tone and Marty were gone, and Tone had left me a note. I was glad she didn't get in the middle of my relationship. She hadn't once said I was wrong for avoiding him. I ripped up the note without reading it and went to take a walk. I peeped through the windows of the empty house where Tone and Mike once resided. There were so many memories there.

I went to sit on the front porch then cried. I didn't stay long because I was too sad. I went in my room and threw away every item, note, or gift that Demonte, or Tone, ever gave me. I didn't want those memories anymore. Those were past chapters in my book of life and it was time to make new chapters. I was tired of being hurt and tired of crying. No more letting people into my heart only to leave me sad and lonely. I knew I would from then on use what I had to get what I wanted no matter the cost.

I was so happy when Lena decided to sell her house and move away. I was ready for new scenery. We moved into some apartments in Midtown. It still was a rough neighborhood, but at least it was more active at night. I had two weeks left in my summer, and I was going to make the best of it.

I sat out on the front steps taking in the night's air.

"Telephone Niyah," Lena yelled from the door.

"Hello," I said as I plopped down on my bed.

"Hi Niyah," Sandra yelled into the receiver. "I miss you girl."

"Me too. I may like this move after all," I said. "It's peaceful here. I'm ready for a new start."

"What about Tone? You're talking as if you're over him completely."

"That's old news honey," I said laughing.

"Did you ever tell him about the baby?"

"No. And there's no need to. I probably won't see him ever again. Enough of that sad news. What's going on with you," I asked.

"Nothing much. You remember Tone's chubby friend?"

"Yeah, the one that sounded like a squeaky toy when he laughed," I asked.

"That's the one. Girl he asked me to go with him to the movies the other day."

"Ugh! I hope you said no."

"Actually, I said yes. He does have a car you know," she said as we laughed in unison.

We chatted a few more hours before I went to bed.

The following morning I awoke to the smell of bacon and eggs.

"Smells good," I said pulling up a chair.

"Eat up. You got a full day ahead of you with your first day at work," Lena said fixing my plate.

"I'm a little nervous," I said.

"You'll be fine. Just take things slowly. And if you have any questions, feel free to ask me," she said.

"Thanks," I said feeding my face.

I was really beginning to see a different side of Lena. Once you got to know her she was alright. She wasn't the motherly type, but she made sure I was taken care of when need be.

After breakfast I dressed and went to work with her. She got me a position as a clerk at James Collins Law Firm office. I loved my job. All I had to do was make copies of important documents and file them into the various clientele folders. He even taught me how to answer the phones and set up appointments.

After I got my first paycheck, Lena went with me to Regions Bank and assisted me with opening my own account. I saved as much money as I could the remaining weeks of the summer. I knew once school started, my hours would lessen. I was beginning to feel so responsible.

Chapter 8


Classes at Central High School were pushed back a week because of a pipe bursting which flooded the cafeteria. It would be a new school, but I was down for the change. One more week of fun was how I looked at it. I became friends with this white girl, Tina, who lived three doors down from me. She acted black and was super cool.

Coming in from work one night I met Terry. Terry lived right next door to me with his wife, Charlotte, and their little boy. I hate to say this, but I met him through his wife. Charlotte was a beautician and would do my hair at her house. She did my hair weekly free because I tended to her son on the weekends. I heard so many stories from her about how her husband was a dog and was cheating with every woman in town. She always said she kept him around for two reasons. He paid all the bills and was a pro in bed. And those were the same reasons I wanted to get to know him.

One Saturday I had her cut my hair into a short bob hairstyle. She was putting the finishing touches on it when he walked through the door. He reminded me of Ginuwine the singer, light-skinned with short curly black hair. His mustache and beard was lined up nicely and only added to a perfectly handsome face. He had two dimples that made my mouth water whenever he smiled. He was also a very nice dresser and smelled great. I could tell he had a ripped body because I could see his stomach muscles through his tank-top. He was wearing loose fitting jeans and timberland boots that made him look tall. And to top it all off, he had green eyes. I was totally speechless when she introduced him to me.

He leaned in as she kissed him on his cheek. When she turned her back, he smiled at me. He sat down at the kitchen table and sorted through some mail as he spoke about his day. Whenever she wasn't paying attention, he would either wink or lick his lips at me. When she went to the bathroom, he slipped me his cell phone number.

"Call me whenever you want me to hit that thang right," he said.

I put the paper in my pocket and sat speechless.

"I'm done girl. Looking cute," she said handing me a mirror.

"You always hooking me up. Thanks Charlotte," I said.

The phone began to ring.

"Terry, let Niyah out," she said going to the bedroom to answer the phone.

As I walked out of the door, he grabbed my arm and pulled me towards him.

"What are you doing," I asked.

"Hush," he said kissing me on my lips.

I was getting nervous 'cause I could hear Charlotte's voice from the other room. I just knew she would walk in and catch us, but she never did. So I allowed him to kiss me for a few more seconds. It was beginning to send chills up my spine, so I pulled away.

"Don't be afraid shorty. There's more to come baby," he said.

"I just bet," I said.

"You'll see when you call," he said rubbing my chin.

Later that night I was horny as hell lying in my bed. I called his cell phone number and heard it ring through the wall. He answered on the second ring.

"I want to test you out to see if you meant what you said previously," I said seductively.

"Okay. I'll be right over," he said.

I then heard Charlotte yelling out how could he leave or go over another bitch's house right under her nose. He retaliated by saying, "Why not? You don't give me any."

I was starting to feel bad because I was the whore she was talking about. But when I pictured his body up against mine, those sad thoughts left quickly. I just knew I had to have him. Charlotte was still arguing with him as he was leaving. I couldn't hear what she was saying so I ran downstairs to the living room to hear better.

I heard her saying that she loved him and didn't know why he treated her this way. He said, "You know my love faded for you when we found out Derrick wasn't my son. You got pregnant by my twin brother. You know that hurt me and tore up my world. The only reason I'm still with you is because I agreed to take care of Derrick when Jerry was murdered two years ago." She was crying cause I could hear her whining. He told her to save her tears 'cause he was leaving and nothing she could say would make him change his mind. He then said, "We don't even sleep in the same bed anymore, and we haven't had sex in over a year." I thought to myself no wonder he cheats on her.

Through our conversations, Charlotte told me she was diagnosed with cervical cancer and that he hadn't touched her since. He got in his car and drove off. She slammed the door, and I went and lay on the couch. I was upset with her 'cause she had messed up my planned night with her husband. She made him mad and he drove off somewhere.

Soon I heard a light tap at the backdoor. When I looked through the peephole and saw his face, a smile lit up on my face. I let him in and didn't ask any questions 'cause I knew he moved his car so she wouldn't think he was sleeping with someone in the apartment complex.

Lena was dating the apartment manager, and she would rarely be at home anymore. Most of her clothes and things were at his place. We would go shopping together, and she would come over a few nights out of the week to eat with me and catch up on things. She told me to bring the bills to her so she would write out checks and mail them off. I kept the place clean, and it was like it was my own place.

Terry was all over me from the jump. He was kissing and touching me everywhere. We stripped and had sex on the upstairs balcony. He was very erotic, and I guess that was what I liked most about him. Whenever we had sex, it would be outside or in the shower so Charlotte wouldn't hear us. On a few occasions we went for a ride in his Lexus. After a while we got bold and would do it right in the bedroom. He was always silent so she wouldn't hear his voice. Although I was the loud one, I never called out his name. She would make fun of me sometimes saying how she heard me getting my groove on. We would both laugh, but I laughed more 'cause I wanted to tell her, "Dummy, it's your husband who makes me scream like that."

I was beginning to not like her much from all the things he told me about her. But she hooked up my hair, and I wasn't about to mess that up 'cause I had to look good at all times. I remember one time we had sex on their couch in the living room with Derrick fast asleep in the other room. She was at her other job, and Terry was supposed to be out playing basketball with some of his homeboys. I got such a rush 'cause we could have gotten caught at any time.

Chapter 9


After a couple weeks of school, I became bored. I was cutting class and hanging out at Tina's daily. I smoked weed and drank almost everyday. I was like a wild child running the streets. I ran into guys and had sex with them on the first night, not even knowing their names. I stopped writing in my journal and I hadn't seen or heard from my mother or grandmother in a while.

Whenever Lena asked what was going on, I'd change the subject. She had no idea I had dropped out of school 'cause she was hardly there. I had turned into those girls Dana and I use to talk badly about in junior high. I had given up on life.

I hadn't even talked to Sandra and we were best friends. I missed talking to her, but I didn't feel like hearing any lectures on why I was allowing myself to slowly crumble. I would often think about Tone from time to time. I was sixteen and living the life of a thirty-year-old.

I thought about how many changes I had gone through my entire childhood. So many different relatives and households I had resided in. I had lost so many friends along the way and attended so many different schools. I was tired of living my life the way others wanted me to. I was going to live my life the way I wanted, with no regrets.

One morning Tina walked with me to school so I could turn in all my books and empty out my locker. Most of my teachers didn't ask questions when I turned in my books. I guess they thought I was transferring to a new school. Ms. Watson, my English teacher, was the only concerned one. Tina stood in the doorway as I entered the class. Ms. Watson was in the middle of a lecture so I just laid the book down on her desk and turned to walk out. She stopped in the middle of her lecture.

"Why are you turning in your book? Are you transferring to a new school," she asked.

"No. I just don't need school anymore. I'm returning my books for some other geek to have," I said.

"Niyah, you are my best pupil. I won't allow you to do such a foolish thing," she exclaimed.

"It isn't your decision. I'm bored with school and I have other things I could be doing with my time," I shouted.

"Well, answer me this one question. How far do you think you will go with an eleventh grade education? You've come too far and to close to graduation to stop right now. Don't throw it all away sweet heart. You're young, and can have fun after you do your school work," she said.

I burst out in laughter.

"Ms. Watson, maybe you haven't noticed but money makes the world go round not education. And as long as you got what it takes to make the dough, then you will prosper. Besides, I got the body and the beauty to make it. Not to mention, the street knowledge. It's some guys out there dumb enough to give up the cash and not even have sex with you," I said.

Ms. Watson grabbed my hand.

"At least think it over. You have so much potential," she begged.

"My decision is already made," I said snatching my arm away.

"Well, let me give you some last words of advice to remember me by. When looks fade away then reality steps in."

"Not my beauty. I'm fine and fit and will always have it going on," I snapped.

"Enjoy it because judging by how tired you look now, you won't last long out there in those streets. And when you realize it, I will be here for you."

*Who the hell she think she is saying that to me,* I thought to myself.

She had no right to judge me, and I sure as hell didn't need her worthless advice. I would be just fine. I had planned to show her.

For the rest of the afternoon, Tina and I lounged around her house, watching movies and eating popcorn. That night I lay in my bed and thought about what Ms. Watson had said. For some reason her words kept repeating over in my head.

*Did I really look that tired,* I pondered.

I ran to the bathroom and starred at my reflection in the mirror. My appearance wasn't that bad, nothing a little pampering couldn't fix. I just looked like I hadn't slept in a few days. It was kinda of hard to sleep while partying as much as I was nightly. I had a few bags under my eyes and my skin was dry, nothing a trip to a day spa wouldn't fix. Tina had given me some eye drops that she said would keep them white and refreshed even if I was drunk and high. I always had gum or breath mints to take away bad breath the weed and alcohol left behind. I would go outside so the smoke wouldn't settle into my clothes or hair.

I reached into the medicine cabinet and applied some drops to each eye and went to bed.

The next morning I took a shower and planned my day. I called Terry and told him I wanted to spend the entire day with him and he agreed. He told me Charlotte and Derrick were going to be gone all day out with some of her friends from work, so we could do whatever we wanted. He took me to Rosie's shop and paid to get my toes and nails done. Then we stopped by Gould's Day Spa, got a facial and deep tissue body massage. The girl behind the counter gave me some tips and samples to keep my skin looking fresh.

We stopped by Exline's Best Pizza in Town and had lunch. I really enjoyed spending time with him. He took me to the Oak court Mall of Memphis and bought me several outfits and matching shoes. We went to a movie that afternoon followed by dinner at Olive Garden. It was late when we got back home and he knew Charlotte would be coming back soon.

"I'm tired of hiding what we have," he said.

"What are you talking about Terry," I asked.

"Look, I know you are young, but I feel we are on the same level. You know what I want from you, and I know what you want from me. I'm willing to give it all to you. I don't love Charlotte, and Derrick isn't my son. I can easily divorce her and we can finally be together."

For a few seconds I was silent. I knew whatever came out of my mouth would change both of our lives forever. On one hand if I said no, I didn't want to be with him anymore he would be upset and probably never speak to me again. Then that would mean no more shopping sprees on him or good sex from him. Honestly, I did care for Terry and enjoyed being with him, but I didn't love him the way he loved me. He pulled up into the parking spot and got my bags out of the trunk.

"I'm not asking you to marry me or make your decision tonight. Just think about it and let me know. And whatever you say, I will do," he said.

I agreed to do so, then gave him a quick kiss and ran up the back steps to my apartment complex. Charlotte was standing on the front stoop as I rounded the corner. I thank God she couldn't see the parking lot from there or she would have clowned. I spoke to her and asked why she was standing outside.

"Terry has been gone all day and he thought I would be out late. I want to catch him coming in with his bitch. I know he has been bringing her here 'cause I could smell her cheap perfume on my sheets. I want to see if he brings the bitch here tonight."

I wouldn't allow myself to go through all that drama like she allowed. She saw my bags and asked to see what I purchased. I showed her as I made up lies about going shopping with some of my friends.

Terry walked up and almost choked on his gum as he saw us talking. She didn't see him at first 'cause she was looking at the contents of one of my bags. I gave him hand gestures to let him know it was okay. He walked right past us and went in the house slamming the door. She excused herself and went inside. I could hear them yelling at each other through the walls. It was bad 'cause she was loud and Derrick was crying. I even heard some things being thrown around and broken. I went upstairs and put my things away. I wanted to go and rescue Terry, but I couldn't without her thinking something. I decided to call his cell phone instead. I could hear it ringing, but he never answered. I was getting nervous 'cause I didn't want anyone to get hurt or have to go to jail. Just as I was getting ready to call him again he called me.

"Baby, are you okay? Come over here now," I said.

"I'm on my way," he said just before hanging up. Charlotte asked him who called him and where he was going in such a hurry. As much money as we pay on rent one would think the owners could have thicker walls, but hell, I enjoyed the conversations as I eaves dropped on Terry and Charlotte. After a few seconds, I heard him knocking at my front door. I knew she was right there with him 'cause I could hear her asking him why he was knocking on my door. I stood there holding the knob in my sweaty palms, dreading what was on the other side. I knew as soon as I opened it some major drama would be going down. I took a deep breath and swung it open.

Terry rushed in past me. The look she gave me was priceless. If looks could kill, the coroner would be hauling my dead ass off right then. Although I was nervous, I stared back at her.

"You bitch. You're the one who has been calling my husband? Have you fucked him? Have you ridden in his car? Has he spent his money on you? Don't you know that he does it just to get in your panties? He's using you like he used all the others. You stupid little skank," Charlotte screamed.

I just slammed the door in her face. For a few minutes she banged on it, then went home and started blowing up both his and my cell. She left numerous nasty messages. I knew whatever decision we made would make things uglier, but I did care about him. Although it took me a while to admit it, I wanted to be his woman.

Charlotte had thrown all his belongings out in the courtyard. He told me he didn't care. He just wanted to leave and get away from Charlotte for good. I told him he could live with me, but he said no. He wanted us both to move 'cause we wouldn't have any peace living next door to Charlotte.

The next day Terry and Lena talked, and she agreed to get all her services and utilities cut off. The resident manager moved us that same day into another one bedroom apartment in the same complex, but on the far side of the courtyard. Later that night we moved all the furniture with the help of his friends. Terry cut the utility services off in Charlotte's place and had them transferred to our new place. That didn't go over well at all.

That night I told him I wanted to be his, and it didn't matter if I was sixteen and he was twenty-five. To me love was blind and had no age limit. We were happy together with our new life ahead of us. Just as he promised he divorced her.

Chapter 10

Charlotte still bothered us at times, but we had changed our phone numbers so she could only put notes on the door and letters on his windshield. She found out our new address when Terry was bringing some groceries home one day. She caught him coming up the steps from the parking lot with bags. He said she came up to him practically begging him to come back to her. She told him how much she loved him and that their son missed him. He said he hated to do the child like that 'cause he was the only father figure the boy knew, but it wasn't his responsibility anymore. He told me she followed him to our door and even asked could she come in and show how much she needed him back in her life, but when he refused she got angry and ran off crying.

When they got divorced I didn't feel the least bit ashamed. *It wasn't my fault she couldn't keep her man happy,* I thought. She had cornered me and wanted to fight plenty of times at the mailboxes, but I told her she shouldn't find it worth fighting for a man who clearly didn't want her.

After about three weeks, I told Terry about me dropping out of school. He was upset, but he said he would take care of me and I didn't have to worry about a thing. In December on my birthday, I turned seventeen. That was also the day I found out I was eight weeks pregnant. I told Terry and he was so happy. The next three months, he was cautious of my doings. He made sure I was taking my vitamins and eating properly. He pampered me all the time. I felt like I had a rare disease instead of being pregnant 'cause he waited on me hand and foot.

In March, during my fifth month of pregnancy I had a horrible run in with Charlotte. I had gotten my driver's license and was driving Terry's car home from work late one night. I had worked over late to help Mr. Collins prepare paperwork for a big case the next day. I knew Terry would be sleep 'cause it was after ten. I pulled up and collected my things out of the trunk. When I closed the trunk, I was looking into the eyes of Charlotte. I guess when she saw the car she figured it was Terry. She probably never expected it to be me. I pulled out my keys and started walking briskly.

As I passed her she said, "Bitch, you gon' just bypass me and not acknowledge me at all after what you did to me?"

"Charlotte, it's late, and I really don't have time to talk to you right now," I said.

She grabbed my arm and turned me around as I tried to walk away. When I spun around my light trench coat flared open and she looked down at my stomach.

"Oh, working on that little family, huh? When is the baby due? I hope you rot in hell you little bitch," she screamed.

I snatched my arm away from her and ran to the steps. She was hot on my trail and grabbed my leg and tripped me up, making me land hard onto the steps. As I moaned out in pain she turned me over then kneeled over me. She stabbed me several times in my abdomen. I never saw her pull out the knife. It must have been meant for Terry, but I caught the wrath instead. I was screaming and fighting with her. She slashed in my hands a few times 'cause I was trying to protect the baby. She ran off into the darkness and left me to die. It was late and I knew nobody would be coming around, so I had to get up somehow. I was covered in blood and my arms and legs hurt badly.

I cried and screamed for Terry to come and help me, but my yells went unanswered. I crawled up the steps and down the hall to our apartment. I lay down in the doorway 'cause I was too weak to stand to unlock the door. I lay back and looked up at the stars and the moon. I prayed silently for God to protect my baby and not let me die right there.

Tina came out on her porch to smoke. When I saw her come out to take a puff off of the cancer stick, I was overjoyed. That was one bad habit I was glad she had. I knew she was my only choice at being saved. I called out her name, and she ran over to me.

"Damn girl. You okay," she asked.

"I've been stabbed," I uttered.

She pulled out her cell and called the police. She took my keys and opened the door, and helped me onto the couch.

"Go and wake up Terry," I shouted.

When Terry came to me he was out of it.

"Baby, what happened? Help me get her up," he shouted at Tina.

He put me in the tub and ran cold water over my stomach. I was in a lot of pain and wouldn't stop bleeding. The baby wasn't moving anymore and I had begun to panic. The ambulance rushed me off to the hospital as the police searched for Charlotte.

I woke up the next day in a hospital bed with my family sitting around me. Sharon, Lena, and my mom were sitting there with Terry. When I opened my eyes and tried to sit up my mother rushed over to comfort me. I looked down at myself and there were IV's in each arm.

The first thing I noticed was my belly wasn't as big as before. I touched it and asked for my baby. Terry came over to me and held my hand. He leaned down and kissed my cheek. I could see something was wrong in his eyes. Everyone was silent and I wanted answers. I yelled out for someone to tell me where my child was because it was obvious I wasn't pregnant anymore. Just then a nurse walked in and tried to push me back down 'cause my heart rate had began to rise. She made me angry. I shoved her off of me, ripped out the IV's, and jumped up. I ran out of the room and toward the nursing station.

"Where is my baby," I asked the receptionist.

"Please calm down. I'll call for your nurse," she said.

"I don't want my damn nurse. I want my child," I exclaimed.

Terry grabbed me and slung me over his shoulder.

"Put me down. What the hell is wrong with you people," I screamed.

He put me down by my room's door.

"I just want to know where my baby is," I asked crying.

"Sweetie, you lost a lot of blood. You're weak, please come sit down," Terry said.

"Not until someone tells me what is going on," I demanded.

"You were attacked by Charlotte coming home from work. The police found her hiding in a closet in her apartment with the knife still in her hand. She admitted she did it and felt bad about it," Terry said.

"I'm glad she was caught, but it still doesn't explain about my child," I said angrily. "Why are you beating around the bush?"

With what little strength I could muster up I slapped him hard across his face.

"The baby died and had to be removed. You happy with the answer now," he asked yelling.

He ran out and left me with a shit load of information to digest. I fell weak to the floor and wept.

After two more days of being in the hospital, I was finally released. Terry came and picked me up and took me home. For the next couple of days I didn't eat or sleep. I was too depressed and hurt. I was angry at the world and didn't want anyone talking to me. I didn't answer the phone or read letters that came for me in the mail. The perfect little world Terry and I had built together was slowly falling apart. We weren't talking and he would stay out all of the time. One night I stood in the mirror naked after a shower and looked at my body. The scars were just about gone thanks to the cocoa butter and prescription cream I had been using.

I lay across the bed and thought about school and everything that had happened to me over the years. I pulled out my journal and started to write. After a few minutes, I turned the book over to go to sleep, but I saw something that made me change my mind. I saw my life flash before my eyes, and I didn't like what I saw. I called Lena and told her I wanted to go back to school.

The next day, Lena and I went back to my old school and had a talk with the principal.

"I'm happy to see you coming back, but we turned your records over to the Truancy Office," Mr. Mitchell said.

"I don't want to be a dropout. I want to make something out of myself," I begged.

"It isn't my decision anymore. Even if I could alter the process, you wouldn't be allowed to come back to this school because you missed too many days," he said.

I began to cry 'cause I knew I had made a big mistake when I walked out of those doors a few months back. I was disgusted with myself for ruining my life. Later that night I received a phone call from Lena.

"I spoke with your great aunt Dora, who works with the School Board. She said she's gonna work on getting you back in school. Give her a call when you can," Lena said.

"I promise I'll do the right thing. Thank you so much," I said.

I called the number Lena gave me right then.

"Hello," a sluggish voice answered.

"May I speak to Dora," I asked.

"This is she. Is this Niyah," she asked.

"Yes mam," I replied.

"Lena told me you'd be calling. Why don't we meet for lunch tomorrow afternoon? We can talk and go over things then," she said.

"Okay. Thanks for your help. Goodnight," I said before hanging up.

Terry was gone out playing ball with some of his boys so I used the car and met her the following day.

Dora still looked the same as I remembered her. She barely recognized me. We ate salad and soup as we reminisced on old times.

"Let's get down to business," she said. "I can work out your record to make it look like you were out on medical leave and get you back in school, but you have to work hard and keep your grades up. It's late in the year, but you can still pass on and go to the twelfth grade and graduate with your right class," she said.

I was happy and astounded.

"I promise I won't let you down," I said.

"In the morning I'll go to Wellington High and register you. Classes will begin Monday morning. Do you think you can make it," she asked.

"Yes mam. I'm determined to get my education," I replied.

"Also, it would be at your best interest to move in with me. You need to get away from all the negative things surrounding you. I've already talked it over with Lena and she said it is up to you to make the decision. You can call me with your answer once you think it over," Dora said.

"There's no need in waiting. I understand what I need to do. I'm ready to move forward," I said.

"That's wonderful. You are a smart girl. Things will be just fine. You go ahead and pack your things and I'll see you tomorrow afternoon," she said.

When I returned home, I felt uneasy. I knew I would have to tell Terry sooner or later.

I planned to break the news to him that night during dinner.

I cooked some pasta and chicken and set the table.

The room was silent. All you could hear was the clanks of our forks.

"I'm gonna move in with my great aunt, and go back to school," I said.

"Do what you gotta do. I don't care."

His words angered me deeply.

I ran to our bedroom and cried. It hurt me that he wouldn't open up and talk to me. I knew he was hurting, but he didn't seem to take my feelings to heart. Didn't he understand that we both lost a child?

I called over Tina and she helped me pack up my things. He never came into the room, even when we carried my things out. He just sat glued to the TV.

"I hope your team at least wins," I shouted at Terry, as I walked past the couch.

I threw his keys and engagement ring to him.

"You have a wonderful life Terry," I said as I exited.

I walked across the garden to Tina's house. I had decided to stay there for the night, so I wouldn't have any drawbacks on leaving the next day.

Later that night, Tina wanted to go out, but I told her I would just sleep 'cause I didn't feel up to it. I lay across her bed with tears streaming down my face.

*Why did Terry turn his back on me the way he did? Doesn't he still love me,* I pondered.

Before I drifted off, I made a promise to myself that from that day on I'd work on me before getting wrapped up into another relationship.

# SECTION 4

A Change Gone Come

Chapter 11

I spent the rest of the morning reading and watching the clock every hour on the hour. Dora said they would pick me up around two so I sat near the door awaiting them. I was so happy and ready to start my new life.

A knock startled me.

*It's them,* I thought to myself.

I got up and peeped through the peephole, and saw Dora and Kema outside. I opened the door and gave each one of them a hug. I hadn't seen Kema in a while. She was two years older than me and hadn't changed much at all. She was still high-yellow with long sandy brown hair. Tina helped us take the bags to Dora's van. I gave Tina a hug and promised to call her when I got the chance.

I turned and starred at Terry's apartment. Something told me to run back to him, but I knew that wasn't the best for me. Kema held the door open while I climbed in. When we drove off, I refused to look back.

The drive was a long one. Dora lived almost halfway across town from Lena's house, which was good to me. We turned into a neighborhood filled with big houses. The streets were clean and the yards were like pages out of a garden magazine. There were no broken down cars or stray animals running around. It seemed peaceful and quiet. We finally came to a stop in front of a huge brick home. I jumped out of the van and marveled at the house and yard. It was perfect I knew I would love living there. Kema showed me to my new room. It was large with white walls and two medium-sized windows covered by mini blinds.

Dora went off to prepare dinner as Kema and I unpacked and put away my things. We laughed and caught up on old times as we put the finishing touches to my room. She was sad to hear the story about how I lost my baby. I raised my shirt and showed her where the scars use to be, but they had all cleared up. She had a few raunchy secrets of her own to tell. She had failed the tenth grade and was in the twelfth instead of being a freshman in college, which she should have been since she was nineteen. After we were done, we played monopoly until Dora called us down for dinner.

We ate and chatted about the rules of the house. Kema and I had chores that were to be done on time with no questions asked. We were to always keep our rooms nice and tidy and keep our grades averaging a "B". We weren't allowed to have boys over unless Dora knew about them. Our curfew was at eleven. Dora was strict, but I needed that guidance to keep me straight.

That night after I wrote a few things in my journal about my move, I cut my light off and got down on my knees to pray.

Kema had a job at a local arcade, and she talked the manager into giving me a job, too. She had a car, so we rode together to work and school. On the next Monday, I went to school. I was nervous since it was my first day. I walked into class and the first face I saw was Sandra. She ran up to me and hugged me. I was so ecstatic to see a familiar face.

"What are you doing here," I asked.

"We moved a few months ago. We live in Esplanade cove."

"That's where I live now with my aunt Dora.

"Cool. It'll be like old times," she said smiling. "Give me your schedule. I'll help you find all of your classes."

The first day went well, and I met a few friends. I really dug this new school and atmosphere. Sandra introduced me to Jovan, whom I found out lived in the same neighborhood. He was a really cool guy. I could tell he really liked Sandra, but she wasn't interested in him or so she said. But I knew better. Jovan introduced me to his best friend Kevin. I remembered him from my science class.

The months and weeks flew by. It was now the middle of April, and we were about to get our report cards. I was a little fidgety, but I felt I did well. I studied day in and out. I got good grades on assignments, quizzes, and passed all my tests. I was relieved when I got straight A's. Dora told me it was in me the entire time, but I needed a change in environment to bring it out. She was right 'cause there was no guidance to make me do my homework or go to school daily. I just did my own thing and nobody seemed to care. Jovan, Sandra, Kema, Kevin and I had become good friends. We all hung out and helped each other with various school projects.

Everyone thought Kevin and I had something going on but there was nothing but a little innocent flirting between us. Besides he had a girlfriend. She was a freshman, but cool in her own way. I could tell she didn't particularly care for me hanging around him, but he made it clear that we were friends, and if she couldn't deal with it she could leave.

Honestly, deep down I liked him, but I couldn't tell if he liked me, so I kept quiet. He always opened doors for the ladies.

That following Friday, Kema, Sandra, Jovan, Kevin and I made plans to ditch class. We all met up at school, then Kema drove us all to the Waffle house for breakfast. We laughed and joked over waffles then went to the mall of Memphis to do some shopping.

Prom was coming up in three weeks and everyone was running around hectically. I had only been attending school for a few months and already three senior football players had asked me to accompany them to the prom. I knew I wanted to go, but I hadn't chosen which one would take me yet. Jovan and Sandra were gonna ride in the limo with Kevin and Kenya so I knew I had to go. They had all purchased their tickets weeks ago.

Jovan, Kema, and Sandra walked off through the food court as Kevin and I searched the various ground floor shops. I already had in my mind what kind of dress I wanted to wear so when I saw the long strapless baby blue gown in the Formal Boutique, I was mesmerized. It had a matching shawl so I knew I had to purchase it. I didn't have any money on me but I found one of Terry's credit cards in my wallet. I tried on the dress and fell in love with it from first sight on me.   I felt a tad bad when I charged that four hundred dollar dress on his card.  I even charged the ninety-dollar matching shoes. We then went into a jewelry store to buy jewelry to top off the outfit.

As we rode the escalators back upstairs, Kevin stood closely behind me.

"What would your girl think if she saw us together like this," I asked.

He didn't reply and I could tell that statement got to him.

"Can we enjoy the rest of our day without bringing up her name," he asked.

"Sure," I replied.

We went into Footlocker and he bought some socks and two pair of basketball shorts before meeting up with the others.

"We can all chill at my house 'til school lets out," Jovan said.

"Cool," we all said in unison.

We picked up pizza on the way. We sat in his living room eating and watching cartoons.

Kevin sat by me and wrapped his arms around me.

"Wanna go in the back room," he whispered in my ear.

"No," I said scooting over.

74

When he moved closer I tried to get up and he grabbed my arm pulling me back down.

"Can I see your room," Sandra asked Jovan.

I looked at her with a frown on my face. She winked at me and followed Jovan down the hall.

"What's up? We're all alone now," Kevin said leaning on me.

"Move," I said pushing him away.

"Stop acting like you don't like it," he said tickling me.

I laughed and we wrestled for a bit.

After a few minutes of fumbling around, he bent down and kissed me. I wrapped my arms around his neck and pulled him closer. I could feel his manhood swelling in his jeans and got turned on.

"I want you so badly," I said moaning.

He unzipped my jeans and pulled off his t-shirt.

Thoughts of our friendship left my mind. I knew us taking this next step would change things between us forever.

A door slamming in the distance jolted us.
I got up and fastened up my pants and jumped back onto the couch.

"What's going on in here," Sandra asked.

"Nothing," Kevin replied.

"Why is your shirt off then," she asked him.

"Um, I got hot," he replied.

I became upset and I ran out to the back porch and sat in the swing.

I bent my knees up to my face and cried. I was tired of feeling empty. I couldn't be mad at anyone 'cause I was causing this pain on myself. I quickly wiped the tears from my eyes as Sandra walked out and sat next to me. I loved being her friend and I had truly missed her being around. We didn't say any words to each other. I leaned my head on her shoulder, and we slowly rocked back and forth.

"What's wrong," she asked.

"Why can't I find someone who actually likes me and is single? I'm fed up with coming second all the time. I feel like a third wheel when I'm around everyone else when they're paired off."

"Don't worry. Niyah, the right guy for you is out there trust me."

Just then Kevin came out.

"Can I talk to Niyah privately?"

"Sure," Sandra said leaving.

"I'm sorry if I embarrassed you. I don't know what is going on or what has come over me. We're good friends, but for some reason I'm, drawn to you in another kind of way. I really like you, Niyah, and I can't help feeling that way. I know I'm with Kenya, but you have to know I was with her before you came along, and now that you're here my world is turned upside down. Either way someone is going to get hurt with the choice I make. But whatever the outcome, I don't want our friendship to end."

I understood what he was saying but I couldn't help feeling like I was going to get the short end of the stick again.

Kema came to the door.

"Come on, girl. It's three. We have to get going before Dora comes home."

I gave Kevin a hug and went back in the house. We collected our things and ran to her car. We had to hurry home to put up our school books and leave back out again to make it look like we came home, but left back out again to go to the mall. That would be the only way to explain the shopping bags we both had. We all said our good-byes in the driveway.

Kevin came up and hugged me again as everyone awaited my response. I was really down and hurt, but I still hugged him back. That was our way of telling each other things were okay. He smelled like baby powder, and he was so warm, I almost didn't want to let go. I got lost in his embrace and I guess he did also 'cause Kema had to blow the horn for me to recognize we were holding her up. He whispered in my ear that he wouldn't mind finishing up what we started earlier. When he tried to kiss my cheek, I leaned back and ran off.

Chapter 12

Kema and I were putting our things away in the house when she asked if I would tell her what happened between Kevin and me. I told her nothing happened.

"I just bet," she said smiling.

Around five, Dora came in with some hot wings and fries from Crumpy's. She said her and a few friends from work were going to a fellow employee's house for a birthday party, in Arlington. And that since it would be late she would just spend the night and come back home in the morning. She rushed off and got cleaned up and dressed. About an hour later she came out lavished in a nice black cotton linen set. She wrote down the numbers where she would be in case we needed to reach her. Kema whisked her out of the door as I went to take a shower. I washed my hair and let Kema blow dry it out and brush it out. My hair had grown back out and was at my shoulders. We ate the food and watched a movie on Lifetime. The phone rang. I answered and was shocked to hear Kevin's voice on the other end.

"How'd you get this number," I asked him.

"Sandra gave it to me," he replied.

A made a mental note to kill her the following day at school.

"Is it okay if I come over? I just want to sit and talk some more?"

"I don't know Kevin."

"Please. I'll just stay a little while," he begged.

"Alright," I said giving in reluctantly.

I gave him directions before hanging up.

I yawned and stretched.

"I'm getting sleepy. I think I'll head off to bed now," I said to Kema.

"So soon," she said sarcastically. "Make sure the neighbors don't see him sneaking in."

I don't know how she knew. I hugged her and ran off to my room. A few minutes later I heard a tap at my window. He climbed in and sat on the edge of the bed with me.

"So, have you decided who you letting take you to the prom," he asked.

"No. Why do you care," I replied.

"Oh I can't worry about a dear friend," he asked.

77

"Now I'm your dear friend? I thought you wanted to get with me now you want to be friends?"

"Whatever," he said pushing me lightly.

"Kenya knows you sneaking in random bedrooms throughout the night?"

"I broke up with her this afternoon. Who cares what she thinks."

His words shocked me. I didn't think he would really do it.

He told me if I wanted he would call her and I could ask her personally myself. I looked into his eyes and saw he was telling the truth. He had done it because he wanted to be with me. I felt comfortable and safe with him and I loved that feeling. He leaned over and kissed my lips. I stopped him and got up and locked my door and cut the light off. We undressed, and then he slipped on a condom from his pocket. He climbed under the covers with me and pleasured my body from head to toe. Afterwards, we laid in each others arms.

"Guess I'll be taking you to the prom since we're together now," he said.

I just cuddled closer to him and kept quiet.

I felt good, but cautious. I didn't want to set myself up for yet another dramatic fall. So I wanted to be sure he meant what he said before he got in my panties again.

"Kevin you say I don't have to worry about Kenya anymore, why is that?"

"I told you I broke up with her. It isn't fair to continue to be with someone when you don't want to be with him or her anymore. I explained to her that it was nothing she did wrong, but that I met someone I totally compared to and wanted to be with. She was hurt, but she understood that it was nothing she could do to change my mind."

"Well, what will she think or say when she finds out it's me who took you away from her," I asked.

"After I finished talking to her she asked if it was you. I couldn't lie so I just said yes. I told her not to be mad at you 'cause you didn't know how I felt. She didn't believe me at first, but I told her I hadn't told anyone about my true feelings for you, which is true. Jovan doesn't even know. She cried, but she's a young girl with a wonderful personality. She'll find someone else who'll treat her like the black queen she is."

I was in amazement to hear his words. They were so real and moving. It felt good to finally find someone to be on the same level with. I thought I had found that with Tone, but I was wrong. Tone had something totally different in mind for him and me. With him it was all about the image thing. He always worried what his friends thought about instead of going off of his heart.

With Demonte, I thought I was his one and only, but I wasn't even gone a week before he moved on. So he was never truly in love with me like he claimed to be. It's hard to tell when you're young and in love or what you think is love.

Now with Terry, it was a little different. It started off as just a fling, but it turned into something much more. I began to long for him near me day and night. I had fallen in love with him. Getting pregnant by him didn't help the situation either. Just when our world was starting to look cozy something bad happened. Now that I sit back and think about it, I don't think we would have ever been at peace with Charlotte living near us. My mother use to tell me everything that happens to you happens for a reason. So in a way I'm glad things happened the way they did, or I wouldn't be where I am right now.

After Kevin left that night, I lay in my bed smiling and thinking about him. I fell asleep reminiscing about what we'd done.

Monday at school, Kenya came up to me and shook my hand.

"What was that for," I asked her.

"The better person won. There's no reason to fight for someone who doesn't want you anymore. Just treat him right 'cause he's a good guy," she said.

I kind of felt a little bad for her, but I finally had Kevin.

The prom was wonderful. We all rode together in a limo and were decked out from head to toe. We danced and laughed and took pictures all night long. Then we retired to a near by hotel, which the senior class had rented out to have a pool party. We drank and ate 'til it was almost morning.

Chapter 13

That following May, Kema graduated. Sandra, Jovan, Kevin, and I were preparing to go to the twelfth grade once summer was over. Kema and I were still working at the arcade together, but I no longer rode with her to school because of her new work schedule. So that meant I had to ride the bus with the others.

The thought of being almost out of school was great. This was my last year in high school and I was going to make the best of it. I had given up on running track, but I joined the volleyball team. I really didn't have much time to spend with Kevin after school, work, and volleyball practice. I could really start to see the changes between us because we didn't talk as much as we use to. But now with school out I figured we could spend more time together. I wanted to continue the relationship with Kevin, but I wanted to feel free to venture out and flirt without worrying about what he thought about it. So what I had decided to do was toy with some of the guys at the arcade. That way Kevin would never find out.

I ate lunch with the same guy everyday. I was operating the bumper cars when he asked if I was ready to take my break. We sat in the back and snacked on a candy bar and drink. We talked about school and what careers we wanted to have. I washed my hands and prepared to get back to work.

We laughed as we walked to the ride area. I spotted Jovan at a video game nearby. He cut his eyes at me and went back to playing. I just knew he would run home and tell Kevin he saw me with another guy. When I got off that night, I was expecting a call from Kevin. It was almost ten and he still hadn't called. I called him, but no answer.

The following morning was a Sunday and I was off work. Later that evening after church Kevin called and asked did I want to go to the movies and that he would be over to pick me up in about an hour and a half. He said his dad let him use the car. I agreed and got ready. We went to the Malco cinema, and then ate at Subway. He never once said anything about talking to Jovan. He held my hand and kissed me as usual. It was like nothing ever happened. But I could tell something was wrong 'cause he never looked me in my eyes.

"You ready to go," he asked. "I'm a little tired."

"Just take me home," I said agitated.

I hoped out once he pulled into the driveway and slammed the door. The next couple of days we didn't talk to each other. We were down to talking maybe a few times a week or every other day or so. I was beginning to become fed up with him.

One afternoon at work, my manager, Mr. Crossen was showing a new employee around. I'd seen this fella' come in a few days ago for an interview and was praying that Mr. Crossen would hire him because he was too fine. I was sitting in the party room with Kema and a few other female employees when they walked in. Mr. Crossen walked him up to each of us and introduced him.

"Hello. My name is Niyah, and I'm so pleased to meet you. It is nice to have another handsome face to look at while working around here," I said walking up to shake his hand.

"I'm Darren," he said.

Mr. Crossen scooted him off and Kema slapped my leg.

This guy was mad controversy. He was the talk of the break-room for the rest of the day. Every time I saw him that day, he would smile at me. He was our new machine technician operator. His job was to fix any of the games and rides when they broke down. I found out from one of my coworkers that he was twenty-three. He was about six feet tall, and had light brown skin. His arms were muscular and I could tell from his polo shirt that his chest was chiseled. He had a deep voice and a sparkling white smile. He had a light mustache and beard and the curly black hair. He could pass for Lorenz Tate's twin brother.

Kema asked did I want a ride home and I turned her down. I was going to ask Darren and I knew he wouldn't mind giving me one. If he didn't then I was up shit creek without a paddle. I was sitting out front on the bench when he pulled up in a gold Mazda 626. He rolled down his window and asked did I have a way home. I told him no that my cousin Kema had left me.

He beckoned for me to get in. He pushed some papers out of the passenger seat and I sat down. It was a nice and clean car with dark tinted windows. I could see myself cruising with him on the town in it. The seats were so comfortable that I laid back and got relaxed. He cut the air on low and slipped in a CD. It was Shai, and the music almost soothed me to sleep. I told him where I lived and we were off. We didn't really speak at all during the ride. When he pulled up in front of the house I got my stuff together to get out.

"No, wait I'll drive you in the driveway and walk you to the door. Wouldn't want anyone hurting that pretty little face of yours."

I smiled.

He got out and opened my door. He grabbed my bag and walked me to the door. There weren't any cars in sight and I didn't have a key. I searched under the flowerpot where Kema usually left it if she leaves out, but I guess she forgot to put it there. Aunt Dora hadn't gotten around to giving me my one yet.

I was a little upset.

"Don't worry, I ain't gonna leave you out here alone," he said.

"I'll be okay. I'll just sit here on the stoop and wait for one of them to come back."

"Okay, then", he said.

Just as if nature wanted revenge, it started to pour down raining. He stopped dead in his tracks and turned and laughed out loud. I laughed as well 'cause now I was soaking wet sitting there in my uniform. It wasn't even rain in the forecast for the day. He ran back to me and helped me to his car. I was shaking and quivering. He cut the heat on so I could get warm. We sat and waited for the weather to clear.

After we were in the driveway for about an hour I had begun to cough and sneeze. He backed out into the street. I didn't even ask where we were going. After about twenty minutes of driving, he pulled up to an apartment complex. He swiped his card and the fence opened to let his car in.

We came to a stop at the back of the units. He ran out and opened my door and helped me out. He put his jacket over my head, and we ran to his door. I stood shyly in the hallway as he locked the door.

"I hope you don't mind me bringing you to my place. I'll take you back when someone returns at your house. I couldn't just leave you out there in the cold."

"That is so sweet of you, and thanks for thinking of me."

He led me to a bathroom.

"Take your things off. I'll bring you something to put on while I dry your uniform."

I handed him my clothes through the door and he put them in the dryer. He brought me back some boxers and a t-shirt. I dressed, and then found him in the kitchen.

"Do you have a towel I can dry my hair with," I asked.

"Follow me. I got some clean ones upstairs," he replied.

He handed me one and I stood at his dresser and blotted my hair.

"Just come back down whenever you're done."

"Okay," I said.

I searched his room, but didn't see anything that led me to believe a female resided there. I walked into the living room, and it was some candles lit and some soft music playing in the background on the stereo. I thought he was slick trying to set a mood.

I walked up to the fireplace and looked at the multiple photos. It was of a small boy with what must have been his parents. I could tell it was him by those eyes and that smile. I heard something in the kitchen and I walked toward the noise. I found him making cocoa. When he saw me, he told me to pull up a stool at the bar. He handed me a cup and a bag of marshmallows. We sat there in silence as we sipped the hot beverage. When we were done, he put the items in the dishwasher. He was such a neat and tidy person.

We were deep in conversation when his clock chimed. It was eleven.

"It's late. Call home and see if anyone is there, so I can take you back."

I used his phone and called home on speakerphone, so he could hear as well. Kema answered on the third ring. I was a little mad but played it off. I told her how Darren had brought me by and nobody was there and she apologized.

"I stopped to get something to eat and forgot to leave the key," she said. "Mom's staying the night over one of her sister's house."

I laughed as she crunched loudly. Darren chuckled also.

"Who is that," she asked embarrassed.

I told her it was Darren.

"The fine guy from work that you been trying to get up on all day? I want details when you get home."

"Kema, you're on speakerphone," I exclaimed.

"It's okay, I won't tell anyone. It will be our little secret," Darren said.

Kema just said she had to go and hung up.

"Since your aunt isn't coming home tonight and we both had to go to work tomorrow, you can spend the night here and after work I'll take you home."

I agreed happily.

He then walked me to the living room and gave me a blanket and a pillow.

"You decide. Do you want the bed or sofa," he asked.

"Where are you sleeping?"

"In the opposite place you choose," he replied.

"I'll take the couch."

"Comfortable choice."

I stood there as he blew out the candles and cut the music off.

*So much for a mood,* I thought to myself.

I watched in amazement as he walked past me into the hallway. He turned and gave me a sexy gaze with his eyes, and I sighed. Then as if he read my mind he came back over to me, but he only said good night and then lightly thumped my nose. I know he could tell I was a little pissed from him teasing me so. He ran upstairs and I plopped down angrily.

After a while I woke up. It was warm under the covers and my skin was sticking to the leather material. I grabbed the sheets and sneaked quietly upstairs. I twisted his doorknob and saw him sleeping. I lay on the floor next to his bed. It almost scared me to death when I turned over and saw him looking down at me from the side of his bed.

"Just couldn't stay far away from me could you," he asked smiling.

"Don't flatter yourself. I came up here thinking it would be better and still can't get to sleep."

"Get up here little brat. You can lay with me."

I hopped up and got in with him. He woke me up after a little while 'cause I was too close.

"Oh, I'm sorry. I'm use to cuddling with my teddy bears," I said.

I scooted back over and fell asleep.

About an hour later I awoke to him closer to me. I turned over to face him and was startled to find him awake. I didn't say anything. I just turned back over, and he pulled me closer. I could feel his body pressing into me. I wanted to jump his bones, but I held my composure 'cause I wanted him to make the first move. After a while he began rubbing my stomach. Then his hands found their way to my breast. I jumped from the sensual way he was touching me. I guess he thought I didn't want him to touch me 'cause he jerked his hand back. I took his hand and led it back to the spot he left tingling. His fingers found their designated place in my candyland. I wanted his lips to take me away, but he never kissed me. Just as I was nearing climax he jumped up and said he was sorry and ran out of the room. I lay there like what the fuck just happened? I waited for him to come back and give me an explanation, but he never did. I finally fell asleep and woke to shower water running.

Sunlight crept through the blinds. I sat up in the bed stretching as I waited for him to come out.

"Morning, sleepy head," he said. "Get up and get ready. We only have an hour to get to work."

Never once did he bring up what happened last night. If he was going to act like nothing happened, then so was I. I got up and put on my uniform. I was in the process of trying to brush my bushy hair when he rushed in and hurried me out saying we really had to go before we were late.

I stomped out the bathroom and down the stairs. He opened the door and I briskly walked to the car. The sun was out, but it still looked like it could rain at any minute. A cool breeze blew across my face as I waited on him to open my door. When he didn't I opened it and slammed it loudly so he would know I was pissed. I felt so used and small. We got to the arcade and I almost hopped out while he was still parking. I was so upset that I didn't even close the door behind me. I jetted into the building without looking back. I clocked in and went to my party room station. I didn't say anything to him the entire day.

When we got off I saw him standing outside his car on the passenger side waiting on me. I walked right past him and hopped in the car with Kema. Before Kema could pull off he sped out of the parking lot furious.

He had no one to blame but himself. I was done with him and his little games. He wasn't going to get the best of me. I wish my brain felt the same way. I thought about him constantly and seemed to keep bumping into him the remaining of the summer at work. Then I thought I would kill him by being nice instead of mean. I would speak to him, and it would catch him off guard.

When we got off work that evening, I saw him leaning against his car waiting on me. I walked with Kema to her car trying to ignore him. Kinda hard to do with him yelling my name to get my attention. And Kema didn't make it any better pointing at him. He knew I heard him. Kema was playing around and wouldn't unlock the door for me. By the time she did, Darren had walked over to me.

He grabbed my elbow.

"Niyah, what is your problem? Didn't you hear me calling your name? I need to talk to you. Let me drive you home."

"Darren, please. There is nothing we need to talk about. You act as if something actually happened between us worth talking about."

The look in his face was priceless. He looked so sad. Damn those eyes of his. I almost wanted to pull him near and kiss him. I excused myself and got in the car and Kema pulled off leaving him standing in the dust. I looked back a few times in the side rear view mirror and saw him still standing there.

We went and ate ice cream from TCBY. When we pulled up to the house I saw his car in our cove. Kema smiled saying that was so sweet how he wouldn't give up on me. It was annoying me and making me mad. But when I saw Kevin, Jovan, and some more boys playing basketball in the street, I thought let me run with this. I hadn't heard from Kevin in weeks. He was watching my every move so I was ready to put on a show. Kevin would pay for the way he treated me.

Kema and I got out and retrieved our things from the back seat. I walked up to the door to find Darren sitting on the porch. He grabbed my things and handed them to Kema and told her I would be a while so go ahead on inside. He pulled my arm and literally dragged me to his car, which was parked near the goal the guys were playing on. He lightly pushed me up against the driver door and put both his arms up on top of the car so I would be trapped between the car and his body. I could see the commotion caught the eye of Kevin. Jovan was yelling for him to pay attention 'cause the other team was scoring on them.

"Niyah please hear me out," Darren said. "I am so sorry for running out like that. It wasn't your fault it was mine."

"You're damn right," I shouted.

"No let me finish, please, baby girl," he said. "When I first met you, I thought, what a loud mouth female. But I later found out that you were okay. I was wrong for leading you on the other night. I got scared, and didn't know what to do. I liked it, but I didn't want to hurt you in any way. I'm not married, and I don't have any children. No, I don't live with or date anyone. I'm not ready for a relationship right now. I have a few female friends, but no one special. So please don't think there is anyone else. I want to continue to be your friend and maybe a little more in time, but I want to take time and enjoy life 'cause I'm still young. I want us to have a thing without labels. I want to wine and dine you, take you out on the town. I want to share and explore things with you like your body if you don't mind," he said, smirking.

I was in total awe of what he had just said. I just gazed in his eyes.

"So what do you say? You want to continue being friends," he asked.

I glanced over at Kevin and saw him watching us intensively. I don't know if it was because I wanted to hurt Kevin for ignoring me these past weeks, or if I really liked Darren, but I told him yes. I agreed to everything he said. We sealed our new friendship with a hug. Kevin got hit in the head with the ball because he was watching us so hard.

"Want to go and grab a bite," he asked.

I was a little hungry and wasn't doing anything else.

"Yeah, just give me a few minutes," I replied.

I ran inside and brushed my hair and let if flow over my shoulders. I went into my closet and choose a cute sundress to slip on.

"Kema, I'm out," I yelled from the hallway.

"Aight," she shouted back.

Darren was still leaning against the car when I returned. I could see we still had a small audience. He opened my door and complimented me as he closed the door behind me. He got in, and we drove off to his place. He said he couldn't let me show him up so he wanted to change as well. I sat in the living room as he showered and dressed. I closed my eyes and imagined his naked body in the shower with the water dripping over his muscles. I began to sweat and wanted to join him. I crept up the stairs and sat on his bed thinking I would catch a look at his body.

He came out of the bathroom in boxers and I was a little disappointed. He just gave me one of those looks like caught you trying to peek a look. I went to his mirror on his dresser and brushed my hair some more. He put on some socks and an undershirt. He walked up on me from behind. He was reaching around me for his cologne. His body was rubbing up against my behind and he knew it was getting to me. I turned around to face him. I closed my eyes expecting a kiss from him and got nothing. He was just looking at me. So I made the move. I stepped up closer to him and put my arms around his neck. When I pecked his chin he put his arms around my waist. He was enjoying himself almost as much as me. But then he stopped.

"I can't," he said pushing me away.

"You are a big tease you know that," I said.

"We're having a lot of fun. I don't want to ruin it."

*How could good sex do that,* I pondered.

We put everything behind us and enjoyed our evening at the movies.

Chapter 14

Jovan was throwing a back-to-school pool party at his house the next upcoming Saturday night. So that gave me one week to break down Darren and have him take me to it.

I went downstairs and waited on him to finish dressing.

"It's a Sunday afternoon, what do you want to eat," he asked.

He looked nice in his neat black Dockers and black polo style shirt.

"Mexican," I replied.

We ended up at El Rio's. We ate and danced to tango music. I had a blast. When he finally took me home my feet were killing me. I saw Dora's car so I knew she was home, but it was way ahead of my curfew. It wasn't even 11pm. He parked in the driveway. It was a clear and warm breezy night. I sat on his trunk as he stood there kicking rocks into the grass.

"What do you think of me," I asked.

"I hate you. I can't stand you," he said smiling. "No seriously, I enjoy talking to you. "You're a wonderful girl once you let your guard down."

He leaned in and kissed me and it took my breath away.

His lips were soft like silk. I would never forget that moment as long as I lived. Just as things started to heat up, he pulled away. I knew what that meant. I hopped down and straightened my clothes. He walked me to the door. I gave him a hug and we parted ways.

I changed into my pajamas and got ready for bed. The phone rung and I thought it was Darren.

"Missing me already," I asked smiling.

"Long time no hear from," Kevin said. "How have things been hanging? No, don't answer that 'cause I saw for myself. Who was that clown you were with?"

"Slow your roll. I haven't heard from you in weeks and you call me with this shit. You can't honestly say you feel we're still together. Kevin I care for you, but you put me through too many changes. I need time to myself to recount things between us."

"I agree with the time and space, but we don't have to break up. I love you and wanted us to work it out. You having sex with him?"

"No, I shouted. We're just friends.

"Well, I don't want you hanging with him anymore."

That pissed me off. I just hung up when he said that. I lay in silence thinking of the fun I had with Darren throughout the entire day. He called me as if right on cue. We talked for a little while before he got sleepy.

"I want to see you tomorrow," he said.

"Cool with me," I replied.

I didn't care what Kevin said, I was going to do what I wanted in the end.

For the next week Darren and I hung tight. If we weren't on the phone we were together.

I asked him to accompany me to the pool party and he agreed. I knew I had to make my move soon because he had to work Sunday and I knew we wouldn't have time to spend together that day. I was starting school that Monday and we wouldn't spend time together as much although he said we would. He picked me up that Friday morning around eleven and we went swim suit shopping at Oak Court Mall. We purchased matching Tommy Hilfiger sets.

We went back to his house to pack our lunch. He got out his picnic basket as I cut up some fresh fruit. He made some ham and cheese sandwiches. I packed our snacks while he packed a small bag of breadcrumbs to feed to the ducks. It was a sunny day, but it was a little breezy down by the riverfront, so I was glad I wore jeans. He laid out the blanket as I sat up our lunch. We munched and chatted. After lunch he wanted us to walk it off. We walked around the trail 'til we got to the pond. We stood near the bank and feed the birds. We then left because he had some errands to run.

Later that afternoon, near the sunset, he took me back down to the riverfront.

"I have a surprise to show you," he said holding my hand.

We walked up to the bridge toward the shore and watched the sunset. I was a little chilly so he wrapped his arms around me. Lights shimmered across the river and set a beautiful mood on a perfect day.

"I wanted to say thanks for bringing happiness back into my life. This week has been the greatest. I'm so use to girls trying to see what they can get out of me. But with you it is different. Even though you have tried to break me a few times. You're simple and I like that. When I'm ready to make that next step you'll be the girl I choose," he said.

I just smiled at him. I leaned in and kissed him. He wrapped his arms tightly around me and pulled me near. We stood there tongue locked as the world went on with its regular routine around us. A few joggers passed us by but we paid them no mind.

"Let's go to my house," he said seductively.

"Lead the way," I said following him to his car.

I thought for sure we were going to get pulled over by the police the way he was speeding home.

We barely made it into the entryway. We were all over each other. Bags and clothes were thrown everywhere. He carried me to his room and made love to me. Afterwards, I fell asleep in his arms.

The next morning, we showered together, and then he fixed us breakfast. We both knew what we did took us to another level and there was no turning back now. We didn't say or speak on what we did the prior night.

He took me home around lunchtime.

"Kevin called you this morning," Kema said. "He said he wasn't feeling well and wouldn't be able to go to the party."

"I wasn't going with him anyway," I exclaimed.

"Girl you too much," she said laughing.

I went to my room and lay down to take a nap. I didn't return Kevin's call.

Darren came by at eight to walk with me to the pool party. He insisted upon meeting Dora. She took a very big liking to him. He had goals and ambitions in life and she liked that in him and thought that I needed people like that in my life to help me stay on the right track. I didn't admit it, but she was right. Although I told her we were just friends she said I hear you, but I see the way he looks at you. That is love in that boy's eyes. I didn't' see anything but lust. It had only been a week since we really got close so I wasn't rushing anything.

At nine we decided to make a late entrance to the party. It was really my fault for taking so long to get ready. Kema had already gone across the street an hour ago.

"I've finally arrived," I said to Jovan at the gate entrance.

He was shocked to see me there with someone else. Darren shook his hand as we entered. He led us to the patio deck. His mother had set up a food table with plenty of snacks. Mostly finger food like fruit, cheese & crackers, hot wings and vegetable bites. She had also set up a drink table that had a variety of soft drinks as well as bottled water and juice. Music was blasting from all over and everyone was laughing and playing around. Only a few people were actually in the pool. I always loved Jovan's yard. They had not to long install a Jacuzzi near the back fence.

As my eyes rounded the yard I saw Kevin and Kenya standing near the stereo.

*He's such a liar,* I thought to myself.

I took Darren's hand and walked around introducing him to all my friends from school. When I got to Kevin I could tell he was a little nervous.

"Hey, Kenya, so nice to see you here. Love your braids," I said. I put on the fakest smile I could find to give her.

"And Kevin, glad to see you're doing well. Kema told me you left a message for me saying you were too ill to come tonight. The power of medicine is all I can say. Oh dear! Where are my manners? Kenya, Kevin, this is my friend Darren."

He shook both their hands and we walked on. I didn't even give Kevin a chance to reply. We ate and drank and danced to music. The night turned out to be a blast even though Kevin was following me around and watched my every move.

Monday at school everything seemed weird. Sandra and I hung together as usual, but the guys hung to themselves. I hated our friendships ended like that, but Sandra and I moved on.

Since I had more time to myself, I began writing again. I had gotten ribbons for poems and short stories I submitted to the school's paper. My English teacher Mrs. White made sure I got recognized publicly. She even helped me fill out college applications. I already knew I wanted to major in journalism and literature. With so much happening in my life I always had something to jot down. Whether it was love, anger, good, or bad, words were flowing out of me like water. Against my will, Mrs. White entered me in a national poetry contest and I ended up wining first place.

Darren escorted me to the prom. I could tell that got under Kevin's skin. He didn't take Kenya like I thought he would. Our senior luncheon was the next afternoon and we were looking forward to going 'cause that would be our last time hanging out as a group before graduation. It was a large picnic at a nearby park.

Sandra got accepted to TSU, and was going to leave in July to stay with family and find a job to save money before school started in September. Jovan got a basketball scholarship to the University of North Carolina. Kevin stated that he wasn't going to college 'cause he would be working with his father at their family shoe store. I had gotten accepted in Rhodes College on a full academic scholarship. My mom framed my acceptance letter and still cries to this day whenever anyone brings it up.

I was the head of the yearbook staff, and I was the salutatorian so I was busy preparing my speech for graduation. Mentally, my plate was full, so I ended up quitting the arcade. Dora had repeatedly given me glory for all my accomplishments I made over the year. I went from being a dropout to being the second best student in a class of over three hundred students. Darren helped me mail out the invitations to my graduation, which was that following Saturday.

As the senior class lined up, I practiced my speech making sure it was right. It helped knowing my family and friends were all in the stands cheering for me.

The whole arena lit up when we walked in to our assigned seats. Flashes of cameras where everywhere as parents screamed out their children names. The first four rows were white gowns signifying honor graduates and the rest of the class were in blue gowns. The principal gave a lecture about our past and future. When he was done, the valedictorian got up and spoke. When he turned to introduce me I almost pissed myself. All eyes were on me and I was nervous. I walked up to the podium and looked out over the crowd. I took a deep breath and read my speech. As I walked away everyone applauded. Tears ran down my face as we threw our caps in the air. We had done it.

**WE HAD FINALLY GRADUATED!!!!!!!!**

# SECTION 5

The Truth Hurts

Chapter 15

After graduation I got a job at a department store. I wanted to save up and purchase a car for when college started, so I wouldn't have any problems getting around when need be. Sandra and I spent a lot of time together before she finally left for school. I was really going to miss her 'cause we were like sisters. Who was I going to talk to when I needed someone to lend an ear? I got her address, and we promised to keep in touch. She said she would come visit on the holidays.

In the middle of July, on one warm evening, Darren and I went for a night run on the river-walk. As we stopped for a breath, he asked would I move in with him. It took me for a total loop 'cause we had never discussed doing that before. I mean I really liked him and we had grown so close over the past year, but that was a big step for me because we weren't dating, and I felt that would create a problem in the long run. I agreed because it would save me more money.

That next week, he helped me pack my things. It was good because his place was closer to Rhodes College, and I still didn't have a car yet. He agreed to let me have his car because he was buying a new truck. He had taken such good care of the car and it was hooked up already. I was rolling big time now.

School had started and I had a job and a car. If I only had someone special to share those things with. I loved Darren, but he never said he loved me. We had numerous conversations about dating, and he always said he wasn't ready. I would lie in bed and cry after some of our talks. He always said I pressured him and he wanted to make sure this was what he wanted. I told him I wouldn't wait on him forever. I just didn't understand why he didn't want to be with me, but he didn't want to see me with anyone else. And his friends were becoming a major nuisance. They always had something to say about us living together. They felt he was a bachelor and I was cramping his style. They would hang out and come over so much and it would get on my nerves. But I didn't say or do anything 'cause it wasn't my place. I just knew I was saving money on the side by living with him. All I had to pay was the cable bill and go half with him on grocery, which wasn't much.

Kema and I grew a little apart because of our busy work schedules. I met Ariel, a girl in my English class, and we started hanging together. She was majoring in accounting and we would help each other out with assignments. She was beautiful, and smart, but had an abusive boyfriend.

We talked on the phone a lot and she would call me whenever he would fight with her. I tried to advise her to leave, but I was on the outside looking in and couldn't relate so I couldn't really change her mind. She felt they were in love and he would change if she stuck it out, which we both knew wouldn't happen. Darren even tried to hook her up with one of his buddies, but she wouldn't go along with it.

That December, Darren finally asked me to be his woman. I think the only reason he did that was because one of his friends saw me out to dinner with a guy from class. Shame it took that to make him move. This upset his friends because their strip club and womanizing days were coming to and abrupt end. He didn't do those things as much anymore and they felt it was my fault. Guess they didn't realize he had what he wanted and there was no need to look when his prize was at home.

I got a surprise on Christmas day. Ariel called me and told me she was pregnant. I was more upset than happy 'cause she was getting deeper into a relationship that she should have been running away from and fast. But I was her friend and supported her throughout her pregnancy. I remember one day when she was eight months along and he beat her up badly for coming home late from work. He slapped her around and pushed her into the wall so hard it left an imprint. She showed up on my porch with a bloody chin. I was crying as I let her in.

She would blame herself for the abuse. She needed help and she knew it, but continued to stick it out. Two months later she gave birth to my beautiful goddaughter Amber. You would think a precious baby would make a man change his ways, but Frank was more abusive because he felt she spent too much time with the baby. On many occasions she would pack up her things, and I would run like a dummy and pick her up and bring her to our house, and by the next day she would be back in his arms. He knew the words to say to make her run back. She thought things would get better, but they only got worse. Before Amber was even one she was pregnant again. The beating never stopped, she just didn't tell me about it as much 'cause she knew I would try to get her to leave him. He would cheat on her with her neighbors in the same apartment complex and she knew it, but did nothing about it. She went into labor in the middle of English class. She was only seven months pregnant when she had Chyna. He had kicked her in her stomach the night before and brought on the labor pains. She didn't tell me, but when we got to the hospital and she had to strip down into a gown. She had a huge purple bruise on her stomach. When the doctor asked about it she told him she fell out of bed. He believed her, but I didn't, I knew how she got it. She always hid the bruises with lies. She would put makeup over black eyes. She could come up with stories that sounded believable, but I knew better.

Darren would try to tell me to stay out of it, but I loved her like a sister and didn't want to see her or the girls hurt. After two years Frank started to slack off somewhat. They didn't argue as much. She had two beautiful girls and was now pregnant again. She was digging herself deeper into that hole soon wouldn't be able to get out.

By the time she had Frank Jr., Darren and I had been together for almost three years. I was twenty-one and in my junior year in college. Our relationship was better than ever, so I thought. He always hung out with his friends, but I never thought he was cheating on me. But my perfect little world was about to take an abrupt change and turn. I was sitting at the computer desk typing a nine hundred word essay for my journalism class when the phone rang. I felt it was Darren.

"Hi baby," I said.

Whoever it was hung up.

I didn't think anything of it. But for the next two weeks it happened day and night. I often told him to get a caller ID box, but he never got around to getting one.

Not until a few times I answered his cell phone and the person hung up on me did I start thinking something wasn't right. The next day, I bought one and hooked it up to the telephone. I wanted to see if the same name would show up on both phones. If so, then they were hanging up because I was answering. This is exactly what happened. He left his cell one night he went to a boxing match with his boys. The phone rang, and it read Keisha Temple, but they hung up without saying anything. A few seconds later, his cell chimed and the exact name showed up on the screen. I was getting annoyed with this person hanging up in my face. I waited about an hour then I called them back. I didn't say anything and didn't have to because she talked first.

"Honey, what is up with you? You haven't come by tonight like you said you would. I've called you numerous times and that bitch keeps answering," the female voice said.

"Excuse me, but I'm that bitch you were just talking about. Who are you," I retorted.

A loud click rocked my ear.

I was raging hot by that time. I called Ariel and told her what had happened and she came right over. She called the girl back and cursed her out over the answering machine. I thought all of this was childish and just wanted to talk to find out some things before I jumped to conclusions. I finally got the girl to speak to me. She told me she and Darren had been dating for a year and a half and they had a son together that was two months old. I listened to everything she said. She had been to this house 'cause she described it room by room. He told her he was in the midst of getting rid of me and moving her in so they could be one happy family. I was so enraged I could have screamed. I told him I wasn't for any games, and to be straight up and honest with me at all times 'cause I was with him. If he wanted to be a player he could have been and I would have still lived here and things would have been great 'cause I would have been dating around also.

She agreed to cooperate with my setup for him. I went and picked her up 'cause he wouldn't come in if he saw her car in the driveway. When I saw the baby in her arms, I got sick to my stomach. He was a spitting image of Darren. He had those mesmerizing eyes. I looked her up and down and wondered what he saw in her. She was fat and frumpy and wasn't even cute. I had to calm Ariel down because she wanted to fight her upon sight. Funny how she was ready to come to blows with this girl but let her man whoop her ass on a daily basis. We all sat down at the kitchen table awaiting his arrival. I set out cracker and sausage snacks for us to munch on while we waited.

I was really shocked with myself. I was holding my composure. Those were signs of being mature 'cause the old me would have went upside her head and his when he got home. I wasn't going to argue, fuss, or fight. I wanted her there, so he couldn't deny anything like most males usually do. She told me all about their little escapades on the town.

After about an hour or so, he called me.

"Hello," I said.

"Hey babe. I'm on my way home. You want me to stop and get you anything?"

"No, you will do," I said seductively.

"Girl, don't be talking like that. You gon' make me wreck. Be there in a few."

"Okay. Bye," I said hanging up.

I was ready to see the look on his face when he saw her there.

97

When he pulled up in the driveway, I met him at the door. He came in and kissed and hugged me as usual. As he hung his coat and hat up, he was telling me about how the guy got knocked out in the eighth round.

"I made a bet with one of my friends and won one hundred and twenty dollars. Here," he said handing me three of the twenties.

I placed the folded bills in my pocket.

"See, I don't mind sharing with you 'cause I love you," he said.

"Oh, really? You love me? Honey let's go in the kitchen 'cause I made you a little snack," I said leading the way.

He followed me although he said he wasn't hungry 'cause he and his boys stopped and got a bite at Crumpy's Wings before coming home. I wish I had a camera to take a picture of his face when he walked into the kitchen.

"Come on honey. Sit down for a minute," I said pulling him by the arm. "Oh, how rude of me. As you know this is Ariel, and this is my friend Keisha Temple, and her darling son Darren Jr. I met her just today seems like she thought she had the wrong number, but when we finally talked we both realized we knew each other better than we thought. You see we share the same man. Funny thing isn't it?"

"Niyah, I'm sorry," he said sadly. "I never meant for this to happen."

He dropped to his knees and wrapped his arms around my legs.

"I love you baby. I love you more than life itself. I was dumb to sleep with her. One of my friends hooked me up with her one night at a club. I swear I only slept with her once," he said begging.

I pushed him away and made him stand up.

"Fuck it Darren. Stand up and be a man. Don't bullshit me. Look at that baby. How can you deny him? Y'all have been hooking up on more than one occasion. I know she's been in this house. You fucked her in the bed I lay in with you night after night. You drag your nasty ass in and make love to me after you probably left her. A whole fucking year Darren? You're good boy. I didn't have one single clue," I shouted.

"Please don't do this Niyah. Don't leave me," he pleaded.

When I wouldn't respond, he ran to our room and slammed the door.

Ariel left and I took Keisha back home. I thanked her for coming over. She didn't say a word to him at all. She claimed she was done with him 'cause he was a liar, but he would pay for his son.

When I returned home he was laying down. I showered and slept on the couch. I continued to live there saving my money, so I could move out when I was done with college. He was happy I stayed, and he promised he would make it up to me. I told him no need to 'cause I didn't love him anymore. He knew the only reason I was there was for school. He would tell me everyday that he loved me, but I wasn't hearing any of that. To quote a lyrical genius, R. Kelly, I was a woman fed up, and there was nothing Darren could do about it.

Everyday he'd have flowers delivered to my job or classes. There would be little notes on my pillow in the evenings when I got home. He cooked surprise dinners and bought me gifts daily. I accepted, but I never said anything.

Three months passed before I let him touch me again. I was going to take his life for a ride and ruin him.

I enjoyed having the upper hand on things. He catered to my needs and made sure I was comfortable at all times. To the outside eyes of our family and friends we were still together. I decided to keep things quiet so no drama would occur. Ariel knew, but it was nothing she could say 'cause her relationship was jacked up itself. Darren had cheated on me and one day he would pay for it.

Chapter 16

I only worked Tuesdays and Thursdays so I spent plenty of time at home. Darren worked ten hour shifts five days a week, so he was rarely there. One Wednesday morning after class, I came home and filled out some online applications and faxed out my resume` to a few jobs. Afterwards, I did a few stretches and changed clothes, then went for a long jog through the complex.

The next six months leading up to my graduation was pure hell. Darren and I didn't spend any time with each other. He worked long days and hung out all night with his friends and I did the same.

He would throw parties on the weekend and all his drunken buddies brought random chicken heads over. I guess he thought I would get mad. I think it hurt him more that I was nonchalant about the whole situation.

After a while, I finally got fed up and left. I packed up all my things and left his key taped to the door. I was ready for a new start.

I had my own place and a new job at a local newspaper company. Sandra had graduated and was on her way back to town. I told her I had a two-bedroom apartment, and she agreed to live with me. I was excited when she moved in. We had a game and movie night each week. We took turns cleaning, and cooking. We split all the bills and shared clothes. We were like sisters once again. Between us both there were plenty of guys running in and out. I had my share of one-night stands and booty calls, but in all I was truly happy with my life.

My mom and I were close again and she helped me decorate my place. Sadly, Sandra and I only lived together for three months. We got into a huge physical fight. It wasn't over money or items, but a guy. I had told her time after time that I didn't like her new man coming around 'cause he would try to hit on me. She said he told her some off the wall stuff about me and him hooking up. I told her he was playing her for a fool and she was too blind to see it.

The evening of the fight I was taking a warm bubble bath when he burst in. Sandra was at work and I didn't know she had given him a key. He locked the door behind him and tried his best to have sex with me, but I fought him off. When she got home, I confronted them both.

"Sandra. I've told you numerous times that I don't want him in my house," I exclaimed.

"I pay rent here. I can have who I want here," she shouted.

"Well, I'm going to call the police. He tried to rape me this afternoon."

"You're such a liar. You want him and you're mad 'cause he doesn't want you," she said.

"What? I can't believe you would say something like that," I said shocked.

She walked over to me and placed her finger in my face.

"I know how scandalous you are," she said.

I pushed her hand out of my face.

"Damn Sandra. I'm your girl. You gone believe him over me? I don't know what's gotten into you lately."

"I knew you were bad news the day I laid eyes on you. I always thought you were a stuck up bitch. I never really liked you, but I did what I had to do to get noticed since boys flocked to you. You were a stupid slut to sleep with Tone while he was with Tawanda. And you were an even dumber bitch to kill your unborn child," she said.

I was so full of anger that all I could do was cry. She had hurt me deeply.

"You get your shit and get the hell out of my house. And I mean now," I screamed.

"I paid my dues for this month. I ain't going anywhere," she said walking to her room.

"Oh! I bet you will sweetie. You just wait," I yelled out behind her as she slammed her bedroom door.

I called Ariel to come over to assist me kicking Sandra out. I needed a witness just in case shit popped off.

Ariel came right on with Frank. Frank used my power drill to take Sandra's bedroom door off the hinges.

"What the fuck are you doing," Sandra yelled. "Get out of here."

"I warned you. You're not going to stay here so you'd better find some place to go and quick," I said flinging her clothes from the closet.

She threw a glass at me from where she was seated near the bed. I grabbed the back of her hair and pulled her onto the floor. We went at it like two alley cats. Ariel jumped in to help while Frank pulled us all apart.

There was a knock at the door. I peeped out the peephole and saw two police officers.

"What's going on mam? Your neighbor called and reported some loud noises coming from your residence," the tall one said.

"Yes, I was about to call you myself. My roommate won't leave. She isn't on the lease and I have proof if you need to see it," I said.

"I want her arrested," Sandra yelled from behind me. "She tore my door down."

I showed them the lease with my signature on it.

"I pay rent," she said as the police read the document.

"Mam, your name isn't on here. You will have to leave the premises," the female said to Sandra.

"I ain't got anywhere to go," Sandra said.

"You should have thought about that before you came at me like that, I said.

"Fuck you," she shouted.

"Fuck you bitch," I said lunging at her again.

"Look, both of you need to calm down. We are going to settle this right now. We are going to stay here 'til you pack up your things and escort you out," the female said to Sandra.

"Make sure I get my keys," I said.

"I don't want them," Sandra said throwing the ring of keys at me.

Sandra and her male friend got their stuff together and left.

After a while a couple of weeks later, crazy things started happening. One morning when I was about to leave for work my car was on four flats. I had it towed and fixed costing me almost six hundred dollars. Another week later all my windows in the car were busted out. That cost me a little over eight hundred to repair. Frank finally talked me into getting an alarm on my vehicle.

Following that, my apartment was broken into twice within the same month. I put in police reports whenever these things happened, but it wasn't much they could do since there were no witnesses. I had rental insurance so I was compensated for all my missing items. I knew deep down in my heart that Sandra was behind it all. Who else would bother me in such a way? Darren didn't know where I lived so I knew it was Sandra.

My mother finally convinced me to move. I moved into a high rise building downtown near the river. Things were tight 'cause bills were all on me, and I didn't have the money to pay them all. I had dipped in my bank account too many times repairing the dumb shit

Sandra was doing to my car. My grandmother and mom sent me money every month to help me out. I knew eventually things would smooth themselves out for the better.

# SECTION 6

Living a Double Life

Chapter 17

When reality finally sets in, it hits you like a Mack truck. You realize you were all alone the entire time. I had lost so many people dear to me over the years. My mom and I were getting our relationship back on track, and I was so happy about that. But she still missed out on a lot of things in my childhood that I wanted her around for. I often sat and thought about how different things would have been if she hadn't gone to that party.

Ella and I never got back to that level we were on when I was younger. But I hadn't spoken to Dana in a long time, and I missed her so much. Whenever I would speak to Sharon, she would tell me that Dana was fine and sends her love. I would give my address and number to her to give to Dana, but I never got a response. I didn't know if maybe Dana was avoiding me or if Sharon just never gave her my messages. I figured it was the latter part because Dana would call if she could.

Tone crossed my mind constantly. I wondered what he was doing and how he was getting along with living across seas, and if he ever thought about me.

I would get sharp pains in my stomach whenever I would think about Terry or Charlotte. That was a horrible part of my life I wanted to push out of my mind. It's hard to do without thinking about the baby I lost. I swear at times I could smell baby lotion and hear a baby cry in the distance. That's one scene I try to lock into the back of my memory. That little body in that coffin. It was so small with embroidered roses all around it.

I saw Kevin a few times, but we never talked or conversed. It was like we never knew each other. Tadarrio still kept in contact with me. It was time to move on and that I did. I didn't want to fall backwards, so I did everything in my power to excel even if it meant stepping on someone in the process.

I would often lie to Ella just to get money and use it to buy things I wanted like clothes and other various items. Anytime anyone came into my life I had to make sure they could offer me something. If they couldn't, then on I went on leaving them in the dust. My whole attitude began to change.

One night, I went to a sorority party with Ariel, and met a Kappa by the name of Angelo. He dressed nice and drove a Mercedes Benz, so I knew I had to hook up with him fast because chicken heads were on the prowl. I went over and we conversed for a while. After the party ended, he offered to give me a ride home and I took him up on it. That night I gave up the goods. The next few weeks, he took me everywhere with him. I went to step shows, frat parties, and barbecues almost every weekend. He kept me laced with new clothes and accessories. I didn't like him at all, but I was quickly falling in love with his money and spending habits. He would sometimes drop me his credit card and let me do as I pleased. I would give him some from time to time to keep him returning. I knew if I didn't some other bitch would.

I remember one incident that happened at an apartment club house Angelo rented for a Kappa party. Everyone was drinking and smoking and having a ball. It was like living the rich life and I was enjoying the ride. That night Angelo asked me to prove I loved him by putting on a dance show for his friends.

"You can keep all the tip money," he said.

"You ain't said nothing but a word," I said.

I could hear the cash register bells ringing as I changed clothes after agreeing to do it. I slipped into a black lace negligee and pinned my hair back. I took two shots of Grey Goose Vodka before I returned to the main area.

The room was filled with drunken Kappas, and I was ready to rack up some dough. Angelo put in a 69Boyz CD as I climbed onto a table. I gyrated as they threw money at my feet. Just as he promised, once everyone left, I was allowed to keep all of the six hundred dollars I collected.

It wasn't until later, that I found out Angelo was a big time crack dealer. He was making mad money and I wanted in on it. I didn't use the drugs, but I wanted to help him distribute so I could get a cut of the cash. He taught me all the ropes of selling and I was on my way. I started out with slinging weed and made a few thousand a week, but I wanted the big bucks, not chump change. He always said I wasn't ready. I was always careful on whom I asked and sold to. I even had a few friends from college helping me. I had refurnished my apartment with new things and bought me a new Wrangler Jeep.

My mom was concerned on how I was coming up with the money and I just told her Angelo's family was rich and he was giving it to me. I didn't want to break her heart and tell her the truth. I was a party animal. My girls and I were clubbing and partying every night and it was starting to show on my face. I had lost weight from not eating, and was back drinking and smoking weed.

I got fired from my job 'cause I would either not show up or be sleep at my desk. Angelo continued to take care of me. He was slowly breaking me down, but I couldn't see it. It started with the name calling and arguing daily. It got to a point where I did actually believe nobody loved me, but him like he said repeatedly.

After four months, I moved in with him. I felt like a secluded prisoner. He didn't allow me to talk to my family or friends. He had become so controlling. I couldn't even go to the store without him asking me a million questions. But the money was good and that made me overlook the bad and stay.

I came home late one evening from a club I snuck to with Ariel, and he met me at the door. He grabbed me by my face and pushed me up against the wall. I was crying and trying to fight back, but I couldn't 'cause he was holding my arms. He slapped me a few times and threw me onto the couch after ripping my jeans off, and raped me. But that didn't run me off. He bought me roses and promised to never hit me again.

One evening, I was cooking dinner, and he came in and trashed everything. He punched me around a few times and left me lying on the kitchen floor bloody. He said he had a bad day and someone had double-crossed his drug money. That still didn't make me leave. Each beating got worse, but the make up gifts got better, so I stuck it out.

I couldn't believe I was the same person who gave Ariel all that advice on leaving a man who hits her and here I was hanging onto one looking for a pot of gold at the end of my rainbow, and only getting lumps of coal with a matching black eye.

One occasion Angelo found a number in my coat pocket. He pushed me down the stairs, and I broke my arm. I was ashamed to even leave the house. I had to sneak and speak to friends or family whenever he wasn't around. I was afraid of what to say or do. I didn't know what kind of mood he would be in that day.

Sex had gotten so horrible with him. He would just take me anytime and anywhere. I felt like a hole in the wall there for his services. I didn't even recognize myself anymore.

Then one day, he surprised me and took me out and wined and dined me all day. He was showcasing me off in public again. He even let me in on selling crack. I had a small area I sold in with a few regular clients. I felt like a queen in a world of luxury 'cause I was addicted to the money.

I stopped smoking and drinking again and thought about my future. I had a secret bank account and I was piling up money big time and Angelo knew nothing about it.

During my stay with Angelo, Darren and I seriously talked about working it out again. Darren seemed sincere and worried about my well being, but I just couldn't go down that road with him again. He agreed I could stay with him 'til I got my own place. One afternoon, Darren and I went out to lunch and a movie. Later that evening when he dropped me off, I told him I would get all my things and meet him at his place.

"You sure you don't want me to stay and help you," he asked.

"No, everything is cool. Go on. I'll be there in a about an hour," I said kissing his cheek.

There wasn't a car in sight so I figured Angelo was gone. The house was totally dark with only the light bulb in the lanterns tracing the outline of the bricked walkway leading my way to the door. I took out my keys and opened the door and closed it softly behind me. I called out for Angelo, but got no answer in return. As I went to click the light on, Angelo came out of the darkness behind me and grabbed me by the back of my neck and threw me face first through the glass coffee table. I screamed out in agony as he pounced onto me. He was trying to choke me as I struggled to fight back. He threw me down on the floor and ripped off my black leather skirt. I was so afraid he was going to kill me by the dreaded look in his eyes. I was crying and screaming at the same time. He was beating me like I was a guy. All I could think about was I was tired and wasn't going to put up with this shit anymore. He rose up off of me to take his pants off and that was when I kicked him hard in his penis with my boots. He dropped down to the floor in agony and that was when I let him have it.

I tackled him down and punched him with all the strength I had. I was biting and scratching him, and he was yelling and pleading for me to stop. I wanted him to realize I wouldn't take anymore beatings from him or anyone else.

"No more", I yelled out with each blow to his head.

The last kick to the face laid him out. I ran and packed my things and hurried them into the backseat of my jeep. But I wanted him to remember not to mess with me ever again.

I went back in the house and walked into the kitchen. I found the biggest pot I could and filled it with water and set it on the stove to boil. I went back into the living room and he was still lying on the floor. I dragged him to the bed. I tied his hands and feet to the bedposts and stripped him naked. He started to wake up and tried to get free.

"Baby, don't do this. I love you. I promise I won't put my hands on you again. I just got mad when I saw you get out of the car with another guy. I thought you'd been cheating," he said.

"I'm tired of your excuses. You're right Angelo. It won't ever happen again. You've robbed and raped me of my life, and I demand it back."

I walked out and checked on the boiling water. I could hear him in the distance whimpering and calling out to me. As I grabbed the oven mittens I thought maybe I shouldn't do this. But when I saw my fuzzy, bloody reflection in the pot the rage took over my body again. Why should I spare him, he didn't spare me? I picked up the pot and carried it to his room.

His whole demeanor changed when he realized what I was about to do. There I stood over him ready to burn the flesh from his body. The next few seconds would name both our fates. If I burned him, I would probably go to jail. If I didn't he'd probably find and kill me. I just couldn't do it.

"I'm leaving. And don't try to find me," I said.

I threw the pot down on the floor and ran out.

"You dumb bitch," he yelled as I ran out the door.

I drove to Darren's house. I sat there crying in his driveway. I had been gone a long time so I guess he was on his way to come and get me 'cause he came out running to his car. He spotted my jeep and ran over to me. When he saw my face he called the police on his cell. He stood by my car until the police and ambulance arrived. They checked me out as I recapped my story to them. They went and arrested Angelo and assured me he wouldn't be able to harm me again because they had been watching his whole drug operation. But they didn't have concrete evidence to put him away til now.

That night, I went to the emergency room and was later released. Nothing was broken. I was just badly bruised. While in the hospital I had a conversation with God one on one. I was in the bathroom when something made me look in the mirror. I almost didn't recognize myself. Both of my eyes were black and puffy. I had several cuts on my lips and each cheek. My mouth was swollen almost shut. I dropped to my knees and prayed that my heavenly Father would deliver me from this life and help me to see the light and do the right thing. I made a heartfelt promise with Him. I vowed that if He would take anyone out of my life that meant me no good that I would do the right things from here on out. A warm feeling came over me and I looked up to the ceiling. It was like God was wiping my tears away. I could feel fingertips on my cheeks. I could hear a faint whisper in my ears.

"My dear child. No need to worry, for you are not alone," the angelic voice said.

That night I slept peacefully.

When Darren took me home, I did just that. I didn't drink or smoke or sell drugs anymore. I cleansed my body with exercise and eating right. I began to look like myself again after time. I got hired on at a local news station to write up reports for the morning anchors.

I found out later that Angelo also had a warrant for his arrest in California. He had been shipped off there, so I wouldn't have to worry about him coming to look for me.        The next day, while at work, I wrote two heart felt letters. One to my grandmother Ella and the other to Sharon. I had a bunch to say to Ella and I felt I could express myself better in letter form than calling her up on the phone.

*Dear Grandma,*

*I just wanted to say thanks for all you have done for me over the years. You have helped me become the person I am. I won't hold you up with all these mushy words, so I'll get to the point. It took me a long time to come around and respect you again. You broke my heart as a young child. You may have never noticed it, but you did. When I came to live with you things were so hard for me 'cause I wasn't around my mom anymore. You taught me so many life lessons, and I appreciate them all, but you also taught me another one. And that was to not ignore other loved ones just because you find love. You abandoned me when Earl came into your life. We didn't talk nor do the things we use to anymore. I felt like the only reason you would include me in things was because I was there not because you wanted to. I was alone and afraid. But now that I look back on it you were in love. Your children were all grown and gone and now you had a child to raise all over again. When my first grandfather died, I thought that I could mend your broken heart by being around and there for you whenever you needed me. But you missed him and were heartbroken. The kind of love a mere grandchild*

110

*couldn't give you. And Earl came and swept you off your feet. I was young and didn't understand what was going on. Do you know how it feels to be pulled out of school in the middle of the year and taken out of town to a new place where you don't know anyone? I didn't have my friends to confide in. Hell, I didn't even have you to confide in anymore 'cause you were to busy making sure your new husband had all his hearts desire. I just held things in and now it is time to let them all go and get on with life. I'm writing this letter not for your benefit, but mine. I needed closure on all these feelings towards you. Don't try to write me back 'cause I didn't address it to my house. I love you and always will 'cause you are my grandmother.*

*Niyah*

I was a little teary eyed upon finishing that letter. I sealed it up and went on to the next one to Sharon.

*Dear Sharon,*

*Bet you never expected to receive a letter from me, did you? It has been a while since I talked to you, and I hope you are doing well. How is James doing these days? Did you ever find that perfect life and marriage you were seeking with him when you cleared the house of Dana and me? I sure hope you did 'cause then it would have all been in vain if you didn't. You know how when you are a little child and you are astounded with someone, and you feel they can do nothing wrong? That is how I felt toward you. I looked up to you. I would say "I want to be like Auntie Sharon when I grow up". Now that I am an adult that has changed. I no longer want to be like you. I couldn't ever turn my back on my children for a man. I could never allow him to abuse them and sit back and do nothing. I wonder how you could consider yourself a mother. A mom is a nurturing person who cares for her young even if it means going without herself. I learned in school that any girl can have a baby, but it takes a woman to be a mommy. I could talk to you and confide in you my girly secrets. You were always an intelligent and sophisticated person in my eyes. But I guess even the smartest individual can have dumb moments. I can't speak for Dana, but it hurt me when you pushed me out. You knew how close Dana and I were and you separated us. Even though you hurt me, I can honestly say, I forgive you.*

*Niyah*

I felt like I had just lifted two heavy weights off of my shoulders when I dropped those two envelopes into the mailbox that afternoon. I didn't tell my mom about what I wrote 'cause I knew she'd talk me out of it.

Chapter 18

The next three years flew by. It was fall my favorite season of the year. The weather was warm and breezy outside, so I decided to go and sit on the back porch and read a book. I had fallen asleep when Darren woke me up. It was dark outside, and he had just gotten home from work. He asked if I was hungry and I replied yes.

He cooked some grilled fish and I made a salad. We ate dinner in silence like we did many nights. It may be hard to believe, but since I moved back in with him he was like a different person. We weren't dating, but he was such a sweetie. He didn't go out on dates with girls or hang out with his friends like he use to. He was always trying to do things with me and I would turn him down. I was there for one purpose and that was to save up money to move out.

I was twenty five and it was time to be on my own and be a responsible adult. I was tired of depending on people. I wanted to stand on my own two feet. He told me on many occasions that he was okay with me staying there, but I wasn't fine with it.

I cleaned away the dishes as he went into the living room and played some soft music. He came into the kitchen and grabbed my hands and led me into the living room. We danced around to Marvin Gaye's "Sexual Healing". I laughed as he lip-synched the words. I missed those times with him, but they were long gone, and we both knew it. I guess he was trying to hold on to them and rekindle something that was dead. I slept on the couch the entire time, so he wouldn't think I wanted him sexually.

After a few more songs I was getting tired. I went to the hall closet and got out my pillows and blanket. He cut up the heat 'cause it was a little chilly outside. He helped me stack up my pillows, so I could get comfortable. He playfully acted as if he was tucking me in like a child. He used his best Mother Goose voice as he told me the story of "Goldilocks and the Three Bears". I smiled the entire time. When he had finished his story he bent down and kissed me on the forehead. Funny how one peck can bring back so many feelings for someone that you thought was truly gone. He leaned in and kissed me on my nose. I pulled him down and kissed him softly on his lips. One thing led to another and I woke up naked next to him in bed the next morning.

It disgusted me that I was weak and fell back down that road again. Having sex with him was the last thing I wanted to do. I didn't want to lead him on, thinking I wanted him back when I didn't. I slowly got out of bed and went back downstairs and fell asleep on the couch. I awoke to the smell of bacon frying. I walked in the kitchen and there he stood at the oven in his boxers preparing breakfast. He looked so sexy. His broad shoulders and muscular legs had me wanting to jump his bones once more. He turned around, and I saw that damn hairline leading down his massive chest and well defined stomach to the rim of his boxers, and my mouth watered. I wanted to make love to him all over again but that would be just as wrong as last night.

He gave me one of his priceless smiles as I sat down at the table. We ate in silence again.

"Niyah, I'm sorry I persuaded you into my bed last night. I didn't mean for it to go that far. I missed touching you and holding you and just wanted to do it once again."

I looked down at my plate as images of last night clouded my mind. It wasn't so bad. We were two mature consenting adults. I wanted no strings attached, and I knew he wanted more than I was willing to give him. I didn't want to hurt anyone or be hurt again. I wanted to make choices for myself. And right then, I didn't want to be with him.

Sex between us was great, but his emotions always got in the way. I wanted to live life with no regrets. I told him I was to blame just as well as he was because I could have stopped it if I wanted to, but I didn't.

He knew I would be moving out soon, and I didn't want to leave any feelings and baggage behind. We both agreed that sex would be too hurtful and ruled it out of our friendship.

After I got off of work that day I went over my mother's house. I pulled up to her townhouse about five. I pulled my coat closed, as I rang the doorbell and awaited her answer. I hugged and kissed her as I always did. I could smell chicken roasting in the background. I hadn't had a home cooked meal from my mother in a while. I set the table as she brought the food in. It was like old times again. I felt like that small child watching her getting dressed in the bathroom. I felt comfortable around her and never wanted it to end. She had come a long way. She was no longer on the pills or addicted to the medicine. She was able to live on her own with occasional visits to a counselor. I finally decided to tell her about the letters I wrote to Ella and Sharon. Although she didn't agree with my words in the letters, she understood why I had to do it. She was the one telling me I needed the closure to go on forward.

After dinner, we sat in the den in front of the fireplace. I sat on the floor in between her legs as she brushed and braided my hair.

"What's on your mind," she asked.

"Mom I want to let you know for a while I was angry with you and hated you for leaving me. I didn't want to live with grandma. I wanted you. That party changed our lives forever. We were so close and it all ended that night you were rushed to the hospital from someone putting something in your drink. Although we talked it wasn't the same. You missed so much. Yeah, you saw pictures, but I wanted you there for me during those special moments. Like my first date and prom. I would often ask God why me? Why was I chosen to live life like this? I was a good little girl yet this still happened to me. I always thought it only happened to bad kids. I often thought that a lot of things that I endured wouldn't have happened if things had gone differently that night. I know it isn't your fault and you didn't choose for this to happen, but I felt like you had control over it and you didn't care. I know different now. I know you love me and always have. I'm sorry if I ever hurt you by my actions or words. I just want our relationship to continue to grow now," I said.

I turned and got on my knees and hugged her. She was crying.

"My dear daughter. You are my heart and always will be. I never wanted to let you go, but I had to. I had to get better so we could be happy again. You have to know I never meant to ruin your life. I tried to be there for you, but it's hard when I can't be with you physically. But we can go from here," she said.

We were both sobbing. We sat and looked at pictures in a photo album. She came across a portrait of her holding me when I was younger. It was such a beautiful image.

"I don't recall us taking this," I said.

"You were too small to remember. Your dad took it. You and I had just moved in our new place. Your dad and I had gotten divorced, but he still came around."

She showed me more negatives he'd taken. She said he use to be a photographer. He had taken so many shots of me as a baby. She never really talked about him in the past. All I knew was he left us. I never even knew what he looked like. She told me whenever I was ready to learn more about him to let her know and she would tell me. I told her I wanted to find him. She was all for it, but told me not to get my hopes up high. She told me the story. He had left her right before I was born. He had an affair with a young girl that worked at his camera studio. When she found out she asked for a divorce. His excuse was he was young and not ready for a family. Even though they weren't married anymore, he still came around and did family things with us. It all ended the day his mistress told him it was now or never for them to go and get hitched. He ran off to Las Vegas and they eloped.

When I was nine, and my mother was rushed to the hospital, he heard about it from a family member and tried to contact me. Ella felt it wasn't the time for that. Mom told me she knew he was back in town 'cause a few years back, she saw him and his wife at a local market. She never told me 'cause she wanted me to be ready to meet him on my own when I was old enough.

How could he live in the same town and not try to reach me? He knew my name and where my grandmother lived, but he never showed up. I was mad and had a lot to say to him. She said he hugged her and was glad to see her, but never asked about me. I wondered why he didn't even question how I was. She showed me a photo of him. He was a tall and handsome man. He was pure Indian with long black hair. I saw that I looked so much like him. We had the same smile and high cheekbones. I saw their prom picture and wondered if he truly loved her. I couldn't understand how he could just walk away like that and not even look back. I still wanted to meet him. I needed that closure from him as well.

One day while driving to work, I heard a radio station posting a lost love ones bulletin. The board was going to be published in the newspaper and on the news station later that night. I called and had his name added and gave my cell number for him to contact me.

Two days later, I checked my phone and he had left me a message. He had a very deep and subtle voice that was clear and to the point. He was happy to hear that I was looking for him after all these years. He stated he had been searching for me and couldn't wait 'til he saw me. I called him and told him to meet me at Olive Garden that upcoming Friday for lunch. I didn't tell anyone 'cause I wanted to do it alone.

I was so nervous the next day when I pulled into the restaurant's parking lot. As agreed, I got our table and waited for him. I knew what he looked like, but he hadn't seen me since I was a child. I was a fully developed woman, unlike the little girl he remembered. My hair had grown out to past my shoulders, and I had colored it a dark auburn color. I felt a lump grow in my throat when I saw him enter the door. The waitress pointed in my direction and I could have passed out as I straightened my jacket nervously. I stood and shook his hand when he came up to me. He hugged me, but it wasn't a tender one. The waitress brought us breadsticks and our drinks that I already ordered for us. He sat then looked me up and down.

"Baby girl, you've grown so much. You're as beautiful as your mother. I missed you so much. I have been waiting for the day we could establish a father/daughter relationship."

"Dad, let's be honest with each other. This meeting is not to start a bond."

Just then the waitress interrupted us asking us were we ready to order or food? I ordered some grilled shrimp and pasta and he ordered lasagna.

"Mom told me the reason you left. Is that true," I asked.

"Yes. I loved your mom and you, but was young and got caught up. I felt pressured into having a family 'cause your mom and I were only married five months before she became pregnant."

"Well, she didn't get that way alone," I snapped.

"I regret leaving, but I felt that was the right thing to do at the time."

He pulled out his wallet and turned to a family photo of him, a lady, and two little boys. He smiled as he told me their names. He even had the audacity to say he wanted me to meet them. The waitress brought us our meals. He began to eat as I stared at him.

"So can I tell your brothers that they will be meeting their big sister soon," he asked gobbling some food down.

The more he spoke the more he made me sick to my stomach.

"Maybe this wasn't a good idea," I said collecting my things.

"Why baby girl," he shouted. "Wait a minute."

People were beginning to look at us.

"Don't get me wrong, I wanted to meet you to get you out of my head. I just wanted to hear from your mouth why you walked out years ago and never came back. I must say you have angered me in so many ways. One, how dare you say you love me and my mother, then in the same sentence say you fell head over heels for some cheap bimbo you worked with. Second, you knew where Ella lived yet you never came by. Mother said she saw you in the market, yet you still never asked about me. And third, you have the nerve to come in here like nothing ever happened, and sit and pull out some damn pictures of some bastards you created with that bitch. And you think I want to meet them. You must be crazy," I shouted.

"Lower your damn voice right now," he yelled. "You're drawing an audience."

I stood up next to the table and straightened my purse on my shoulder.

"Well, I'm glad to see you don't want to ruin your reputation. Let me show you the one thing I learned from you," I said as I walked out.

I sat in my jeep and cried. Not tears of pain, but joy.

I called my mom on my cell and told her what happened and she laughed. She said I acted like Ella. When I told Darren, he felt I was a little harsh. But he was glad I was feeling better.

The following morning at work, I made a new friend. She was there through an internship program. One day at lunch, I let her proof read a poem I wrote about my dad, and she felt I should enter it into a national poetry contest 'cause it was just that good. After days of her riding me about it, I finally did. And shockingly, I won first place, the prize was five thousand dollars. I had finally found my calling. Everyone was so proud of me. With my money I put a down payment on a new house. Ella always told me to establish some ground and put my cash to good use. And what better way than this? As an early house-warming gift my mother gave me a copy of that picture of her and me. She had it framed and put it in a beautiful white box with little purple butterflies on it. I was so glad of the direction my life was finally going.

Darren was sad that I was in the process of moving out. I had already gotten the utilities cut on, and furniture delivered to my house. Darren was a sweet heart and really helped me out. I would be moving in the next day, but I didn't want to leave without setting things right between him and me, once and for all.

I fixed a surprise Mexican dinner that night. When he came home, I had the lights off with candles everywhere with soft jazz music playing in the background. We ate dinner and afterwards went out on the patio. We sat looking up at the moon and stars.

"Darren I want to thank you for being there for me through it all. You are one of my best friends, and I will never forget you. You will always be in my heart just not the way you would like. I love you don't get me wrong, but you truly hurt me when you cheated on me. You ripped my heart out and stomped on it. You were the last person I thought would hurt me in that way. We seemed perfect together. Things happen for a reason, and I believe that. Maybe this was to show me that there was something else in store for me. You are a great man and will make someone happy someday. Don't waste your heart or time on me 'cause I'm not the woman for you. We will always be friends though. I'll come by and we can go to a movie sometimes. But I don't want us to ruin anything by adding sex into the mix again. I think things are best this way."

He never said a word and I knew deep down he understood all I said. He finally tapped my shoulder and said he truly was sorry for all he'd done and that he would take it all back if he could. That night we lay in bed fully clothed and cuddled up together.

The next morning was a big day for me. I moved the rest of my things to my new place.

*Home sweet home,* I thought as I flopped down on my couch.

# SECTION 7

The Presence

Chapter 19

The phone blasting in my ear woke me up. I looked around and it was dark outside.

*Dang, how long was I sleep,* I pondered.

It was almost eight and I still hadn't finished cleaning my desk off. The phone rang one last time before my voicemail picked up. She was just checking on me to see if I needed help. I called her back.

"Hi dear," she said.

"Sorry I missed your call. I was busy," I said lying.

"I got someone on the other end, but I just wanted to let you know that Dana will be landing at ten in the morning, so make sure you're there to pick her up. Also I'll cook dinner for you all later tomorrow night."

"I will. Thanks ma," I said hanging up.

My mother finally talked Sharon into giving her Dana's contact information. She then passed it on to me and I called Dana. We laughed and cried for hours on the phone before Dana agreed to fly out and visit me the following week.

I had taken the next two weeks off to spend time with Dana. I had a whole agenda that we would go by during her stay.

I lit some candles and requested Alexa to play my cleaning playlist. Jill Scott's vocals echoed off the walls as I relaxed in the tub. After a while of soaking, I changed into my pajamas and jumped into bed. Just as I was falling off to sleep, the phone rang yet again. I adjusted my eyes to focus on the digits on the screen. It was Kema. She'd gotten my number from my mom.

"Hey. Long time no hear from. What are you doing girl," she asked.

"Sleeping," I said sluggishly.

"Oh no! Get up and go to this new lounge with me."

"I'm tired. Why don't we do this some other time," I insisted.

"No. I'm gonna keep calling back if you don't say yes."

"Okay. Okay. Damn. You still haven't changed," I shouted.

"Glad you saw it my way," she said.

She gave me the directions and I hung up.

I stood in front of my closet, deciding what to wear. It was chilly outside although it was the beginning of fall. I decided on my hip hugging black leather skirt and a tan turtle neck. I pinned my hair up and sprayed on some perfume. I slipped on my knee high black leather boots and out the door I went. I played my Nicki Minaj Queen cd as I cruised down Union Avenue, toward Club X. Kema had given me her cell number and told me to call her when I was there. I parked my jeep across the street in the parking lot and slowly walked towards the line that seemed to never end at the club's entrance.

It was a huge building with blue and green neon lights flashing everywhere. The thumping of the music from inside had me feeling good. I called Kema and she instructed me to walk to the front of the line and give my name. The fat bouncer stopped me, but when I said who I was he lifted the ropes and let me in.

*Kema must have some clout in this place,* I thought to myself.

When I got inside, it was dark except for the blue lights that were on. As I walked through the hallway, guys tried to grab my hand, but I just kept on strolling past them. Leaving the scrubs to only wonder how being with a queen like me would have been. There weren't any tables, only a few booths in the back. There was a huge dance floor in the middle of the room that was already full to capacity with people grinding all over each other to Cardi B's song Money. I stood there taking in the scenery before I finally made my way to the bar and sat down.

Two hands covered my eyes from behind.

"Guess who," the deep voice asked.

"I don't have time for games," I said. "Just tell me who you are."

I got annoyed when they wouldn't say anything else.

I pushed there hands away, and when I turned around it was Jovan.

"Hey boy," I said jumping up to embrace him.

"I spotted you when you walked in. You wanna join us at the table," he asked.

"Sure," I replied.

I walked with him over to his booth. That is when I saw Kevin and Kema. I hugged Kema and sat down next to her. Kevin and I caught eye contact a few times, but we didn't speak. Kema ordered me the same drink she was drinking. I didn't want to get drunk so I just sipped on it for a while. I ate on some hot wings as Jovan and Kema went to the dance floor.

"So how have you been," Kevin asked.

I rolled my eyes at him over my apple martini.

"I'm good.  How are you and Kenya doing," I asked.

"Come on.  Let's not go there tonight please.  You're looking good," he said changing the subject.

"Thanks."

"You wanna dance," he asked holding his hand out.

"No.  My feet are hurting in these boots."

Just then this fine ass creature of a man came over and whispered in my ear for me to join him on the floor.  I took his hand and followed.  The look Kevin gave me was fierce.

"My name is Matthew.  What's yours," the fine creature asked.

"What?  Oh my name is Niyah," I replied as I peeped over his shoulder at Kevin.

I guess Matthew sensed something was wrong.

"Your attention seems to be elsewhere," he said leaving me standing there in the middle of the dance floor alone.

Kevin walked up to me.

"You're here so let's dance," he said.

I turned to walk away from him, and he pulled me back.  He looked damn good in his navy blue turtleneck and baggy jeans.  And his cream Polo boots was giving off a major thug appeal.  He smelled of Versace cologne.    Thank goodness fast songs were playing, so we didn't have to be close.  We both loosened up after a few jams.  We were having so much fun that it didn't even matter that it was going on midnight.

Kema finally talked me into ordering another beverage.  I ordered a Tequila sun riser.  The sweet and sour taste had me buzzed.  The DJ came on the microphone and said the next song was for lovers.  The slow beat of "It Seems like You're Ready" by R. Kelly blasted through the speakers as couples ran to the floor.

"Let's go and sit this one out," I said.

"Come on.  Just one last one," Kevin said smiling at me.

I was tipsy but I reluctantly agreed.

He wrapped his arms around my waist and pulled me near.  I relaxed my arms around his neck and we stared deeply into each other's eyes.  Some how the drunker I felt the finer he got.  He bent down to my ear and sang along to the song and it was beginning to turn me on.  If we were any closer we would have been one person.  I rubbed the back of his head as he sniffed and rubbed his lips along my cheek.  When he made it to my lips we kissed.  I took his bottom lip into my mouth as he moved his hands down to my butt. I could feel his penis swelling up against my leather skirt through his jeans. Kema bumped me from behind on purpose and we stopped.

I looked at Kevin and came back to my senses and ran off to the table and gathered my things to leave. Kevin was running behind me and caught up with me at my jeep.

"What happened? Did I do something wrong," he asked.

"You know what you did. I'm not going there with you so let's end it now."

"Don't leave me like this," he said pointing to his crotch, which was still a little on hard.

He took my hand and walked me to the passenger side of my jeep, which was near a brick wall.

"Let me feel you one more time," he begged.

"Kevin, I don't have time for this. We might be seen anyway, so no."

He pushed me gently up against the door, and guided his fingers up my skirt. He rubbed my vagina through my lace panties. When I became moist enough he slipped them to the side and slid two fingers deep inside my candyland.

"Seems like you ready," he said leaning into my ear.

He was right. I opened the passenger door just incase anyone walked by. He pushed my skirt up above my butt. I slipped off my panties and sat down on the seat with my legs hanging out. He took my left leg and rested it up on the handlebar as he dove face first into my vagina. His tongue was soft and warm to the touch. We had never done anything like that before, so I guess some woman had turned him out over the years to my present day pleasure and expense..

I was glad when I finally climaxed 'cause Kema had called my cell twice. When I saw her come out of the exit door through my window and head that way I hurried him 'cause I knew she would freak to find us in such a compromising position. He licked up all my excess juices and I hurried and straightened my skirt back down just in time. Kema was headed our way as he wiped his mouth with the back of his hand.

"You okay," she asked me.

"Yeah. I just had something to do and Kevin was walking me out. I'll hit you up later okay?"

She looked back and forth from Kevin and me. I knew she knew something happened 'cause she just kept giving me this look like yeah right. She hugged me and whispered in my ear that she wanted all the details 'cause she knew something went on. I laughed loudly as I pushed her away. Kevin gave me a piece of paper with his number scribbled on it and asked me to call him. I got in the driver side as he stood at my door. He kept sniffing his top lip and smiling at me. I knew he wanted to finish what we had started. I thought about it for a minute then I balled up the paper and gave it back to him.

"Sorry, I don't back track", I said as I crank up my jeep and drove off.

I left him standing there pondering over what just happened.

I fell asleep that night grinning to myself. Kevin would be thinking about me for a while. I led him on and left him high and dry. And I wasn't the least bit bothered by it. It was good, and I didn't regret letting him do it. At about three in the morning I was tossing and turning. Candyland had a mind of her own. She was twitching and yearning for some dick. I picked up my phone and dreaded that I didn't keep Kevin's number.

I picked up my cell and scrolled through the contacts. One of the first names I came to was Darren. He didn't answer so I left a message saying for him to come by if he got this within the next hour.

I turned back over and closed my eyes.

I heard a car pull up to my house after about 30 minutes.

I got up and peeped out the window.

Darren hopped out of his car in what seemed like night clothes. I knew he had jumped right out of bed and came right over.

I rushed down and opened the door.

"I saw you called," he said smiling as he leaned in the doorway.

"Whatever. Come on in," I said.

He followed me back upstairs to my room.

He was telling me about his day at work when I threw him down on the bed, and took his shoes off. I didn't say a word as I undressed us both in less than two minutes. It didn't take much to get him in the mood. A few kisses and nibbles here and there seemed to hit the spot. I expected a quickie, but didn't get that at all. We did almost every position known to man before he reached climax. He had me so sore I was beginning to regret calling him. We went for another round then collapsed in each other's arms.

When the alarm went off at eight the next morning, I jumped up quick. He was still lying next to me. He wanted to go out for breakfast, but I told him I had other plans for the day and that I would call him later. I let him take a quick shower with me which was a mistake cause we ended up having sex again. I was pressed for time 'cause it was already ten minutes after nine. I dressed quickly and we both left.

I arrived at the airport at about a quarter to ten. I parked near the walkway leading to the main lobby door. When I saw Dana's little round head, I got happy. She looked the same. Her hair was short and curly, and a light-brown color. She was still tall and skinny. When she saw me she dropped her carrier bag and ran to hug me. We laughed and giggled like schoolgirls. I stacked her things in my trunk, and we drove off. She was recapturing her flight as I pulled into my garage. After she unpacked and got settled in the guestroom, she came downstairs. I cooked us breakfast. We ate turkey sausage and Colby cheese egg white omelets as I caught her up on my life since I last saw her. We laughed and cried as she caught me up on her life's drama as well. She ended up putting her daughter up for adoption. She wasn't ready to raise a kid. I understood. She was raped, and never wanted to keep the baby in the first place.

After I cleaned the dishes, we went to the Wolfchase Galleria Mall. A full day of shopping makes a girl tired. I ordered grill chicken and pineapple pizza and we lay at the end of the bed and watched movies on Lifetime. The next morning, we went for an early morning jog down by the riverfront. We had dinner at my mom's house that evening and spent the night there.

Wednesday, Kema invited us to another dance night at Club X. I was glad that Kevin wasn't there to bother me. We danced and drank all night. Some guy tried to get Dana to go home with him, but she wasn't going for it. She was dating a famous football player back in Atlanta, name Vince. She told me all about Vince and how great he was to her. He played for the Atlanta Falcons. They had been dating for a while and she anticipated marriage in the upcoming year 'cause he had proposed to her. She said whenever I came to visit her in the peach state she'd hook me up with one of his football friends.

Thursday we went site-seeing on a boat ride and that night we went to the Grand Casino in Tunica to play and eat dinner. The days flew by. Although we had been apart we were still close and promised to keep in touch. I hated to see her go 'cause that meant back to the real world again. Back to work and on with the track of things.

Chapter 20

I dreaded the week ahead of me as I entered the doors of Literary Resources and Associates. I was the leading journalist and back behind my desk typing away. The holidays were coming up, and I would be alone. My mom and her new boyfriend were going on a Christmas cruise in the Bahamas.

I called Dana and set up a flight to Atlanta for December 21st. I was happy when the day of my flight came. Dana picked me up from the airport. She marveled at the change I did to my hair. I had cut it all off to a low Halle Berry pixie cut, with burgundy highlights to accent it.

"I love it. It brings out your hazel eyes," she said, rubbing her fingers through it.

Back at her house, I helped her decorate her tree and put lights up around the outside of the house. We were like kids playing around in the snow. We were ducking and dodging behind cars in the neighborhood as we pounded each other with snowballs. Small children were watching us out of windows probably thinking how silly we looked all grown up playing around like fools. We made snow angels and a huge snowman before finally freezing and going back inside to warm up.

While we were preparing dinner, Vince called and said he was coming over. I prepared the salad as she put the finishing touches on grilled chicken breast and sautéed garlic potatoes.

Vince was just as she described him. He was tall with broad shoulders. He was a big and a very handsome man. He put you in the mind of Gerald Levert. I didn't watch much football, but I remembered his face from a TV commercial. She seemed so happy with him and they looked good together. Her dreams of having a good husband and some kids were coming true.

"I have a friend I want you to meet," Vince said to me.

"That would be great," Dana said.

"How ugly is he," I asked Vince.

"Girl, stop it," Dana said, slapping my arm.

"Okay. I'll meet this mystery man," I agreed.

"I'll set something up later this upcoming weekend," Vince said.

After dinner, they went to a movie, as I watched TV and fell asleep on the couch.       Vince had a game that upcoming Sunday, and he gave me and Dana two box seat tickets and back locker room passes. The game started at three, but he wanted us there about two. Without planning Dana and I dressed alike. We both stepped out in the hall in burnt orange turtlenecks and hip hugging jeans. We stood side by side in the tall mirror in her room marveling at our attire. We winked at each other and decided to go dressed alike. We still had similar taste in fashion. We were a bad combination. I learned that the night we went to the club when she visited me. We laughed as we slipped on our black leather jackets and got in her truck. I loved her black Infinity truck Vince bought for her last birthday.

The highways in Atlanta were different from Memphis. People down there drove fast. You'd better either get with it or get the hell out of the way 'cause you would get your ass ran over. She zipped in and out of traffic like a pro.

We pulled up to the stadium and parked in the back lot. We walked up stairway after stairway making it to the stadium entrance. We looked like chics right out of the matrix with those black long leather trench coats and light orange tinted shades on walking side by side, daring a bitch to step out of line. Atlanta brothers were bold and we were surely turning heads. They would be with a girl and still turn and give you a compliment. The girls only looked us up and down. We only smiled and marched on.

We finally reached the skybox and it was perfect. There were only a few seats in there. Nobody ran back and forth bumping your seat on their way out or blocking your view. Only businessmen were seated with us. We had a waitress that came in and catered to our every need. I wasn't a football fan, but put me in front of a basketball game and I'm just like one of the dudes. It was cool, and Atlanta seemed to be a good team. They were playing the Chicago Bears. Dana screamed as her boo did his thing on the field.

I was checking out each guy on the team wondering which one he was going to introduce me to. They all looked nice from where I was seated, but they had on helmets, so I couldn't really see their faces, but physique wise they all pretty much had it going on. There was this really arrogant player, number thirty, that kept dancing around whenever he made a touch down. I kept my eye on him 'cause he had a nice ass. Atlanta won thirty-one to nine and the fans were going wild.

About an hour after they won, a young male came and got us and walked us down to the locker room. We had to wait 'til they dressed and were interviewed. My heart lumped up in my throat as we got closer

128

to the locker room entrance. Vince greeted us at the door. I told him good game as Dana jumped into his waiting arms. There was a sea of blackness floating around the room. Some of them were shirtless while some were dressed. I saw the number thirty jersey lying on the bench next to a guy who must have obviously been the cocky wide receiver from earlier. Most of the guys were circled around him. He had his back to us and was shirtless. He had a perfect muscular back. He had a bulldog tattoo with T-Dog printed under it along his shoulder blade. He had a deep voice, but I couldn't make out what he was saying. He was hand gesturing out a play he made during the game.

"T-Dog, come here for a second. Got someone I want you to meet," Vince yelled to him.

He never turned around. He slipped on his shirt and got up.

When he finally walked toward us, my mouth dropped to the floor. Talk about your past coming and kicking you in the ass.

*Are my eyes playing tricks on me,* I pondered.

There I was standing face-to-face to Tone, and he didn't even recognize me. He still had the smoothest brown skin and his face was just as I remembered it. That same white smile was sparkling brightly. He was more handsome now than then. His head was shaved bald and he had a full beard and mustache.

So many things were racing through my mind at that moment. He was looking me up and down and I was watching him through my shades.

"Damn baby girl. You got it going on in those jeans. You make me wanna sing like Ginuwine," he said grinning. "My name is Antonio, but everyone calls me T-dog."

"Or Tone," I said.

He gave me this weird sideways look.

I slowly slipped my shades down, revealing my face. He stared at me in disbelief for a few seconds.

"Oh my God. This is the Tone you were talking about? Isn't this a small world," Dana said.

I excused myself and walked out.

I couldn't face him or this situation right now. I went to the women's bathroom and washed my face in cold water. I couldn't believe what I just witnessed.

I figured you came in here," Dana said breathing profusely.

"I can't do this. I need to get out of here," I said.

"All of that y'all went through was in the past. Maybe he is over that now," she said. "At least give it a chance. Who knows?"

I dried my face and we walked back to the locker room. Tone was leaving out with his bags. He came over to me and shook my hand.

"Sorry, but I got to be heading off. It was nice to see you again though," he said as he walked off.

And just as fast as he had entered back in my life he was gone again.

Dana tried to get me to follow him but my feet were stuck in what seemed like cement. I couldn't move if I wanted to. As his body got smaller in my eyes view, I wanted to kick myself.

"Don't worry. We all go to the same place every time we win. Come with us and maybe you'll see him there," Vince said to me.

He drove off in his silver Mercedes Benz as Dana and I followed in her truck.


Dana and I kept on the same clothes. We pulled up at Wild Bill's Sports Bar and it was packed. There were cars and groupies everywhere. Females were there thinking they could get up on some money. I walked through the doors expecting wild scenery, but it was calm and laid back. There was light music playing over the speakers as the game was being played again on the big TV screen. It was dim and there were people filed into booths like flies, anticipating being near one of the players. Tone and a few other guys were waiting for Vince at a back secluded booth, which was larger than the other tables.

When we walked up, I saw a white girl hugged up on Tone. It enraged me, but I didn't show it. I wondered why he was all checking me out earlier and wanting to get to know me better before he recognized who I was when he had a snow bunny at home. Vince, Dana, and I sat directly across from them.

"What's your name," the white girl asked me.

"Niyah," I said giving her a fake smile.

"I'm Tammy," she said moving closer to Tone.

She looked like a cheap hooker. Her hair was blonde and hung down her back. She needed some tips on her makeup 'cause she looked like a clown. She noticed how I kept eyeing Tone and gave me a sly smirk.

We sipped drinks and ate hot wings as they all chatted about the game. I was tired of being bored, so I got up and walked over to the jukebox in the back choosing some more songs to play. I was bent over flipping through tracks and didn't notice anyone had walked up behind me. They pressed their body into my behind.

"Excuse me," I said moving over a little without looking up.

"The pleasure is all mines," the soft masculine voice said.

When I stood up and looked him straight in the face, I noticed we had an audience watching.

"What did you just say," I asked.

"Don't apologize for putting that sweet ass on me," he said smiling.

"So you did it on purpose?"

"Yeah. That's why I came over. I saw your banging ass from across the room and I had to come and touch it to see if it was real or a dream."

Now I realized he was young and had an ego, but he had no right to be rude, and disrespectful. I walked up closer to him and played along with his game. He had never met a girl like me before, and I would make sure he never forgot me either. I took his hand and placed it on my butt.

"You like that big boy," I said seductively.

"Hell yeah," he shouted.

"Oh you do? Then what are you waiting for? Come and take it."

When he moved in closer I put my finger on his lips teasingly.

"Do I look like that kind of girl?"

He sighed and made an angry face.

"You'd better jump on this now while I'm still interested in you. I'm a rookie on the Atlanta team. I'm sure you've seen me on TV," he boasted.

That comment drew cheers.

Dana knew I had control of the situation so she just sat back and watched the show instead of sending Vince to say anything.

"You better watch yoself," Tone said. "She's a feisty one."

I had to put this chump in his place.

"Excuse me then for being so rude. What clout or rank you got on the field? This is your first year on the team right? Do you actually get a chance to enter the game and play, or just warm the bench up for the real pros? Boy, get your two dime ass out of my face before I make change. On your best day and on my worst day I'm still too much woman for you," I said.

"I don't know why you tripping. You know you want this," he said grabbing his crotch.

"Me want you? Get it straight. You came up to me not me to you. What do you have to offer me that I don't already have, sweetie? Please don't say money, cars, and house, 'cause I got all that. You need to realize I'm not one of these chicken heads you see up in here nightly," I said walking off toward the table.

Dana and I high fived as I sipped my drink.

Tone winked at me as the entire room burst out in laughter. I was tired and ready to go, but I could see Vince and Dana weren't ready to leave. I went outside and sat on the trunk of Vince's car. It was cold so I pulled my jacket up around my neck as I looked up and admired the stars above. I heard footsteps and was almost afraid to look around. I just knew it was that rookie from earlier coming to kick my ass. I turned to find Tone walking towards me.

"Why you sitting out here in the cold," he asked.

"I just wanted to clear my head."

"Same old Niyah. Spicy, just the way I remember you. I knew you would put him in his place. You have to do them like that 'cause they feel cocky especially when we win. But in his defense, you do look good."

"Thanks," I said.

"Sorry I ran out earlier, but I just didn't know what to say to you. I do have something I wouldn't mind asking you," he said moving closer.

I stopped him right there.

"Look Tone. I apologize for avoiding you like that when you were about to leave for Germany. You have to understand I felt it was the right thing to do 'cause I didn't want you to go. I couldn't stop it so I didn't want to be left hurting in the long run. So why not end it to keep the heart ache down," I asked.

He rubbed the tear away from my cheek that began to fall.

"It didn't take the hurt away 'cause I didn't know what was going on and I thought about you all the time. You always crossed my mind. I loved you."

His words were cutting me deep, but I deserved them. I never got to say goodbye to him.

"Whose world you rocking now," he asked as he playfully jabbed my shoulder.

"I'm not in a relationship."

"You ain't getting any? That's hard to believe," he said.

"I got booty calls. Just no man. What's up with you and the fake Barbie?"

"Don't do that," he said frowning.

I heard her call his name from behind us and he walked away. She ran up and hugged him.

"I was so scared 'cause I couldn't find you. I wondered what happened to you," Tammy said kissing him.

I watched as they walked back into the Sport's bar.

I went back in and sat with Dana. I saw Tone and Tammy grinding on the small dance floor. I was getting a little annoyed.

*He ain't my man so why worry about it? It's a party so let me get loose,* I thought to myself.

After a few minutes, I was searching for them, but Tone and his bimbo were missing and I figured they left. I drank and danced my little heart out. I was starting to get sick and needed air. Dana gave me the keys to go sit in her truck. I fumbled and tumbled over my feet as I made my way to it. I heard a low whimper noise. I didn't know what it was, so I hurried and got in and locked all the doors and peeked out of the passenger side window. I had to try to adjust my eyes to focus on what I was seeing. I wasn't dreaming. There was Tone and Tammy having sex doggy style up against the back of a car. I watched him in amazement. He was giving up the dick that use to belong to me. As I watched them I had to admit I was getting horny. All those memories of us making love came flowing back. I wanted to go and kick her tramp ass to the ground and jump on him 'cause she obviously couldn't take it like I could from all the screaming she was doing. I guess he felt me watching, and turned in my direction. When we caught eyes he winked and slowly licked his tongue across his lips as he kept on pumping. He glared at me the whole time as if he was showing me what I was missing. He knew what he was doing, and I was falling deep into his trance.

That night, I dreamed about him pleasing my body outside under the night's moon.

# Chapter 21

On numerous occasions I came and visited Dana and they would throw barbecues and pool parties. Tone would rub up against me whenever he walked past. We would sneak a hug and kiss from time to time. He knew I wanted him, but he would act like he never knew me whenever Tammy would come around. He would do just enough to get me going then leave me high and dry and leave with her.

One evening during a pool party I went inside the house to get a fruit tray when he came in behind me. We were all over each other in the kitchen when Dana came in and caught us. He went back outside and she just looked at me.

"I don't want you to get your feelings hurt," she said.

"I'm grown. I know what I'm doing. Neither one of us are married. We're just having fun fooling around," I said.

But Dana was right. I was hurting on the inside. It tore me up how he could say he still loved me and wanted to be with me, but never made a move to get away from Tammy. I couldn't blame him 'cause I was stupid for making myself available to him. I would fall for his words and let him get a quick feel when Tammy wasn't around. I felt so low and dirty, but knew one day he would come around.

Although Dana, Tammy, and I hung out, I still envied her 'cause she had my man. I didn't want to compete for him, but you can't tell your heart what to do when it has a mind of its own. I thought about him constantly and wanted to be near him.

It was becoming expensive constantly traveling back and forth from Memphis to Atlanta. Dana finally persuaded me to move there. She was right, I was young, and Atlanta had more to offer me job wise. It took me two months to sell my house. I sold it to a nice lawyer and his new wife. They thought the house was exactly what they needed to start a family. I gave all my old furniture to Ariel and turned my two weeks notice in. The last visit to Atlanta, Vince helped me find a nice uptown condo. I had already moved some things there, and Dana had helped me decorate. I was ready for a new outlook on life. I bought a beautiful chocolate suede coach and matching love seat set. I found some Japanese artifacts that would go great with my furniture. I bought a nice bedroom set that had large spiral iron black posts. Dana knew how much I loved Tigers, so she bought me a black silk sheet set and a tiger striped duvet. She even made me drapes to hang over the bed poles. The room had a very sexy feel to it. I was sad to leave my friends and family behind, but I was on to bigger and better things.

Tammy hooked me up with an interview where one of her friends worked. It was a major magazine corporation. I had a promising conversation with the boss, who was ecstatic to see me after the raves she heard from Tammy. She said from right off she could tell I would fit in great from just my style of clothes and look alone. And checking out my resume` and references only put the topping on the cake. When I got the offer call to accept the job, I flew in the next day to Atlanta with the rest of my things. I didn't even tell Darren I was leaving. I would write him and let him know what happened. I started work that following Monday, so I made sure that I was in my place on Saturday to get settled in.

Dana threw me a huge housewarming party. Picture a football team giving you gifts. Vince had called all his friends together and told them I was moving down there. It was Sunday, and they knew I had food and a big screen TV. They wanted to watch the football game that was scheduled to come on since it was their team's bye week. Tammy had the party catered by her mother who owned a catering business. If it hadn't been for her sleeping with my man, I would have actually liked her. I couldn't help, but think that maybe she was doing these nice things to keep tabs on me. If she was with me then she knew Tone wasn't.

Everyone had arrived and was downstairs. When Tone and Tammy walked in, I tried to stay occupied. I was feeling bad, but didn't show it on my face. I went upstairs to put away some of the gifts. I was placing some candles Vince had bought me that were tiger stripped on my fireplace ledge when Tone walked into my bedroom and sat on my bed.

"This is soft. We could do some things on this," he said patting my bed.

I just rolled my eyes and never turned around. He was talking out the side of his head, and he knew it. Our flirting had not gone further than groping and kissing. I stepped back and looked at my room. I had hooked it up nicely. The wall to wall carpet matched the chocolate walls.

To the left as soon as you walked in was the fireplace. Dana had bought me a large picture of two Bengal tigers lying near a creek, and I had it hung over the mantle. I had a vase with black and orange feathers in it next to the new candles Vince bought me. There were a few pictures of friends and family spread along the wall as well. Robert, one of Vince's teammates, bought me a velvety Chanel logo designed blanket with two matching pillows to put down in front of the fireplace. He said that was for a night we would sit and sip hot cocoa on a cold day. I told him that sounded nice and I'd let him know when he could come by and do it. Robert was a nice guy that I met on one of my previous trips there. We had become phone buddies over the past few weeks. Dana told me he liked me, but I never took her or him seriously. It was nice to know someone admired you from time to time.

My queen sized bed was made up with black silk linen and plenty of soft pillows. The silk drapes and tiger striped drapes Dana made for my bed poles were draped like a tent and gave it a romantic look. I had candles everywhere to set a tranquil and romantic mood.

My mom bought me a stack of earth sound CDs. She knew how much I loved the sound of water while I relaxed. I could see Tone was watching me out the corner of my eye as I walked around the room and straightened up things.

I walked over to my picture window and watched the rainfall. He came and sat down on the ledge next to me.

"You remember that night in Lena's window when I made love to you," he asked.

"Yes," I said gazing into his eyes.

The look of lust he gave me had me on fire.

I wished I could clear out the house and make love to him one more time. I would make him ever forget he knew Tammy. I wanted him to remember what he was missing as well.

*"Why did I ever let him go,* I pondered?

I know I didn't have control over him leaving the states, but we could have ended on good terms and that way no matter who was in his or my life we would know we were truly in love once.

I knew Tammy would start missing him, so I decided we should go back downstairs to keep her from coming up here catching us. He was rubbing my feet in his lap as we sat and looked out the window. This was nice and I wanted this to be a daily thing. I drifted off into a fantasy. I could hear the music playing in the background to our beach wedding. We looked happy as we floated off on a cruise to Fiji for our honeymoon. I could see us living together and having kids. But those were just my dreams and they probably would never come true. I just kept dazing in his eyes hoping he could somehow see what I felt for him and tell me to be his for life. All I knew was my heart overflowed for him and I wouldn't rest 'til he was mines.

I knew Tammy was a user. Dana said they had been dating for a few months, and she'd been spending his money big time. Just as he was beginning to massage my calve muscles there was a knock at the door.

"Tone, you in there," Tammy asked.

He quickly jumped up and ran over to the fireplace to make it look as if he was looking at photos.

"Come in. It isn't locked," I said sadly.

She came in and marveled at my room. I just watched her as she ran around and touched everything. She then hugged him from behind.

"You need to let me redecorate our bedroom," she said to him.

It was hard to conceal my anger, so I jumped up.

"Can you two leave? I'm not feeling well," I said.

"Sure," Tammy said leading Tone by the hand out the door.

I slammed the door behind them and lay across my bed. I balled up into a ball and cried myself to sleep. I awoke to Dana rubbing my head.

"I missed you downstairs and wondered what happened to you," she said.

"I was just tired and wanted to take a nap," I said stretching.

I looked at the clock and had only been asleep for about thirty minutes or so.

I got up and straightened my clothes back out and followed her downstairs. The party was still going strong. They were yelling at football plays on the TV as they munched on hot wings and beer. Dana was doing a good job at keeping the house clean as they ate. She walked around with the trash can and broom to catch anything that fell on the floor. I made mixed cocktails handed them out to everyone as Vince put some music on the stereo.

Everyone was coupled up with girls Tammy brought with her. I walked past them and out to my screened in patio. I slipped out the door and lightly closed it behind me. I took two small tea light candles and a bottle of wine and a glass with me. It was a little windy but it still felt great to me. I could still hear the music and people laughing and it made me angry again. *How they dare they be happy when I was so down,* I thought to myself.

My tranquil state of serenity was broken by Robert's interruption.

"I saw you sitting out here from the kitchen window and decided to come out and join you," he said sitting down. "Can I sit with you for a bit?"

"Sure," I said.

"Has anyone told you that you have beautiful eyes," he said as he slipped off his shoes and socks.

I watched him with no answer.

He had a body chiseled like a piece of art. He had short dreads and a peanut butter complexion. His green eyes, juicy lips, and low cut facial hair had my mind in a trance. He reminded me so much of the actor Michael Ealy. We sat talking for a while.

"You seem like a great guy. Why aren't you dating anyone?"

"I choose to be alone. I dated around a few times, but never found a decent girl to take home to momma."

He lightly punched my shoulder as I burst out in laughter.

"I'm serious," he said. "What about you?"

"I'm too wrapped up in my work to be in a relationship."

"You deserve to work and play. You have to make time," he said.

"Well, I don't so let's drop this conversation please," I exclaimed.

He took his index finger and traced the outline of my jaw.

"If you give me a chance, I can teach you how to do both," he said.

"Really," I said seductively.

"Let me show you," he said turning towards me.

He leaned over and kissed my cheek. I turned my head towards him and we tongue kissed. The sweet taste of his tongue made the hairs on the back of my neck stand on end. His hands were everywhere and I wasn't about to stop him cause it felt too good. I turned to the side, and caught eye contact with Tone in my kitchen window looking out at us. I could see the anger in his eyes through the windowpane. Robert began caressing my breast.

"Let's go upstairs to my room," I moaned.

"Thought you'd never ask," he said, as we got up and walked back inside.

I excused Robert and I from the party and told Dana to lock up when they were done and Robert and I retired to my room. We wrapped up in the velvet throw he had bought me for my housewarming gift as we had sex. The entire scene was so romantic. He made love to me like I was his wife. He moved slowly and made sure I was enjoying myself just as much as he was. Afterwards we fell asleep in each other's arms.

For the next few weeks, we hung out daily. We weren't dating, but close friends. We would go out to eat, and to the movies. He was into the same kind of stuff I was, and it was great to relate to someone on the same level. I continued to go to the games with Dana to see Robert play. I was beginning to really open up and like him, but I wasn't ready to take that next step. Things were going well so why mess it up.

The girls at work didn't know what to think. I was getting flowers and gifts delivered to work everyday. Tone saw me hanging with Robert and wanted to show that he cared also. He sent me presents on my birthday and Christmas which were both in December. He even sent me a dozen roses on Valentine's Day. I told Robert everything, so he wouldn't be shocked and he was cool with it. Tone continued to stay with Tammy so I didn't take his words or actions to heart. He wanted me to run up behind him although he didn't have any intentions on being with me. I was tired of those games, and I was going to let him know.

It had been a year, and things were still going the same way. Robert and I still were kicking it. I let my hair grow back out to shoulder length 'cause Robert liked it that way. Robert and I were meeting up at Vince's house for a grill party. I pulled up and walked into the house to find Robert all over some chic grinning from ear-to-ear. I walked on in and helped Dana with the food.

"Don't worry girl. She doesn't have anything on you," Dana said trying to calm me down.

"I'm fine," I said lying.

I knew me and Robert wasn't dating, but it was a respect thing.

I helped Dana serve the drinks. There in the middle of the leather sectional in the den, was Tone with Tammy sitting in his lap like he was Santa.

"Niyah. Did you meet my friend, Elise," Tammy asked.

"Can't say I did," I said as I handed Robert his drink.

"I wanted to hook her up with a nice guy and the first person that came to mind was Robert. I figured it would be okay. You two aren't dating are you," Tammy asked.

I smiled a big fake smile and stayed quiet.

"He doesn't have any rings on his finger. He's free to make his own decisions," I said.

I glared at Robert angrily as I walked by, and he followed me to the kitchen.

"You okay with the situation 'cause I had no idea 'til I got here that she was trying to hook me up with that girl," he said.

"Robert, I'm cool. I'm tired and about to leave anyway."

"Can I go with you then?"

"No. Go and have fun with your new friend."

It had begun to rain and everyone was coming inside.

I grabbed my things and ran for the door.

"Leaving so soon," Tone asked. "The party's just beginning."

I didn't reply.

"Hope it wasn't something I said or did," Tammy said laughing.

"You know what? Before I leave I got to get a few things off of my chest," I said as I walked over to Robert.

"You're a good guy. You send me to work with a smile on my face every morning. I ain't mad at you, a man can't help it when a thot throw themselves at him," I said looking in Elise's direction.

She didn't say anything, and believe me I was waiting for her ass to say a word so I could put my foot down her throat.
I then turned to Tone.

"Look, I know you still care for me, but I can't keep playing these games with you. You are all over me when Tammy isn't around and tell me you want to be with me, yet you never make a move. You know she is a gold digger, yet you stay with the bitch anyway. You know where I am come find me when you are ready to rekindle that love we once had," I said.

Just then, Tammy jumped up, and I stopped her dead in her tracks.

"Sit down, bitch, before I take a straight pen to your fake ass."

She turned crying to Tone as I walked out the door.

I ran down the path to the lake behind Vince's house. I needed to clear my mind before I drove off anywhere 'cause I was too angry. I stopped and stood at the dock overlooking the lake. It was pouring raining and my hair was sticking to my face. My clothes were drenched, yet I stood there. It was cold, but I didn't mind 'cause the rain hid my tears. Just then I heard some branches crackling in the distance and I quickly turned to face Robert. He must have seen where I was headed. I fell into his arms and cried.

He held me tight as if he could understand my hurt and pain. He grabbed my face and kissed me gently on my lips. I begged him to fuck me right there and he did.

Afterwards, I walked to my car and he went back to the party. I drove home and sat in my tub filled with warm bubble water. Jill Scott soothed my ears as she sang through the ear buds of my IPod. I must have dozed off 'cause the next thing I remember was jumping to a noise I heard coming from downstairs. I took my towel and wiped my face and listened for it again. It was a knock at the door.

*How long was I sleeping,* I pondered.

I wrapped a towel around my naked body and opened the door to a drenched Tone.

"What are you doing here," I asked.

He pushed right past me without saying a word. He picked me up and carried me to my room where we made sweet love all night long. We fell asleep, and then I awoke to him gone the next morning. I figured he felt bad about what happened. Little did I know he'd broken up with Tammy that same night. Dana had left a message on my phone saying that Tone and Tammy had it out when I ran out on the party.

I called her back and told her what happened.

"I can't believe you and Tone hooked up. What are you going to do now," she asked.

"I don't know. It's up to him. If he wants to get back together then I'm all for it. Look, I'm a little tired. I'll hit you back later," I said before hanging up.

When I washed up and went downstairs to fix me something to eat, I found a note on my table.

*Niyah, I love you and always will. There's no denying that. I want you in my life so get ready cause I won't rest until you are.*

Those few sentences made me happy on the inside. I finally had my man back and things would be great again. New place, new job. Things were looking great. This move was great for me. We would take things slowly this time.

# SECTION 8

## Hello Motherhood

Chapter 22

For the next few weeks things were going great. Dana and
Vince were still going strong with their relationship. They were looking
forward to getting married this upcoming fall. I was helping with
making arrangements. She was nervous, but I told her there was nothing
to worry about 'cause she would be beautiful and nothing would ruin her
special day even if that meant I had to be security at the door. She was
marrying the man of her dreams. When I said that, it always calmed her
down.

Robert was back to his player ways. He called me on a few
occasions, but I told him I couldn't go back to us having sex. I was
building a future again with Tone. He understood and didn't cause any
problems for us. Tammy left a few crazy messages on my phone, but
once Dana and I went to her job and had a semi threatening conversation
with her the phone calls stopped. Funny how telling someone you would
rearrange their face, so badly that their mom wouldn't recognize them
can make them leave you alone.

I loved my job. I had written many articles in our new Fashion
and Love Line Magazine, Urban Trends. My boss put me over the
project of reaching the younger crowd.

Tone and I were finally on track. He would meet me at my
office for lunch, and we'd go out to eat in fine restaurants. Tone and
Vince took turns having parties at their homes entertaining guests. It was
like a dream being with Tone again. We both had changed so much over
the years, but not our love for one another. I really hated that I threw
away all his notes and letters in the past, but I had new love items to
collect now. He was always giving me cards just to say he cared.
Flowers were delivered to my office every Friday afternoon. We had
become inseparable. Every Sunday, I was in the skybox yelling right
along side Dana for my baby as he ran yard after yard. The Sunday
evening after they put a hurting on the Cleveland Browns, I threw a
cook-out. Tone had run four touchdowns and they won fifty-six to
seventeen.

Everyone met up at my house following the game. I was
bringing a platter of fish in from the deep fryer when I got dizzy and fell

to the floor. Tone ran and picked me up to see if I was alright. I told him that I was fine and I just hadn't eaten anything for the day. I figured once I sat down I'd feel better.

I was okay until we were dancing around on the patio. My head started spinning and I threw up. I didn't know what was going on. I hadn't drunk but a little gin, and I ate a few pieces of grilled salmon. Tone made me go and lay down. He was right. I was pushing myself and needed to rest. Little did he know I was getting sick like this daily for the past two weeks. I would get sick at work and have to walk out of important meetings before hurling on the projector.

Dana said I was pregnant, but my cycle was so off track lately. And I had been stressed. I didn't know whether to worry or not. The next morning on the way to work I stopped at Walgreen's and bought an E.P.T. pregnancy test. I left it in my office bathroom while I went and gave a presentation in the conference room.

I was nervous, but I had to represent a new layout for Urban Trends. After the meeting I ran back to see the results of the test. I had the receptionist hold all my calls and I locked my door. I took my linen jacket off and pranced around the room before breaking down and looking at the small tube. I held it in my hand with my eyes closed. This could change my life, and I wanted to be ready for whatever it placed upon my plate. I opened one eye to a plus sign. I dropped it on the floor and sat down on my couch.

I thought back over all the symptoms. I didn't know whether to be happy or sad. I touched my stomach trying to imagine the little life growing inside of me. Tears began to flow. God had blessed me again with a child, and I was going to keep it this time. I wasn't ready in my life for a baby, but I wouldn't make a rational decision without letting Tone know this time.

A tap at the door broke my special moment. I picked up the box and contents and placed them in my top desk drawer. I used a Kleenex to clean my face.

"Who is it," I asked, walking toward the door.

"It's me mam," the receptionist said. "Tone is in the lobby waiting with some Chinese food. Do you want me to send him in?"

"Yes, just give me a minute."

I had forgotten we had planned to have lunch together.

I put my jacket back on and straightened out the wrinkles in my knee-length linen skirt and sat down at my desk. I crossed my legs and put some papers in my hands to look as if I was busy. He came in with a

144

big smile on his face. He was in such a good mood, and I was not feeling well after seeing the positive pregnancy test.

He brought in the bags and set them down. He handed me three red roses.

"Here baby. I thought you'd love these," he said.

"Their gorgeous," I said smelling them.

I cut the stems and just as I was about to put them in a vase I tried to pull them apart so they would stand right, I noticed there was something holding them together. Tone watched closely as I struggled to arrange them. I turned the blooms over and saw the most beautiful platinum diamond ring attached to a pink ribbon. I slipped it off the stem and held it in my hand marveling at its beauty. When I looked at him he was down on one knee.

"Niyah I love you and want to grow old with you. Make me the luckiest man in the world and marry me."

He took the ring and placed it on my finger.

"When you catch your breath you can give me a yes."

I just continued to sit speechless.

It was romantic and I tried to fake a happy mood, but he saw something was wrong. He came around and sat on the arm of my chair.

"You okay," he asked concerned, rubbing my back.

I pulled out the drawer and handed him the E.P.T. box. His eyes got bucked and watery. I could tell he was nervous by the way he was opening the container.

"Now, Tone, do you still want to marry me after seeing this news," I asked.

"I'm going to be a daddy," he shouted.

He was so excited.

"I'm not a hundred percent sure. I'm gonna make a doctor's appointment to have a blood test done," I said.

"Let me know when and I'll go with you," he said, still staring at the tube.

I stood up to take my jacket off 'cause I was getting hot again. He patted and talked to my belly like the baby could actually hear him.

"Have you thought of any names yet," he asked.

"Tone, calm down. We don't know if there is a child."

"Well, are you going to give me a straight answer now about what I asked earlier?"

"Yes. Of course I'll marry you," I said, smiling.

He grabbed me and held me tight.

I took off the rest of the day and we relaxed at home. Not too long ago I was trying to get him to notice me. Who would have thought that two months later I'd be his fiancé and we'd be sitting in a doctor's office awaiting a pregnancy test? He was holding my hand tightly. You would have thought he was going to get some heart breaking news from the look on his face. He was sweating lightly, and it was making me even more nervous. The lobby was small yet cozy. There was a small television in one corner that had a baby delivery program on it and a table with a tower of maternity magazines spread across it in the middle of the room. There were newborn baby posters all over the room. A few of the women in the lobby were pointing and whispering. I knew they recognized him from TV. My man was famous.

Who would have thought that the big head stubborn guy from my past would be such a star now? If someone would have told me back then that things would have turned out the way they did, I wouldn't have believed them at all. I flipped through a brochure as we waited on the nurse to call my name.

"Mrs. Sutton," the nurse yelled out.

We both hopped up.

He insisted I used his name. Why, I don't know. We followed the short, stubby nurse to a small room at the end of the corridor. She told me to undress and wait for the doctor to return. I sat on the edge of the bed in a paper gown.

"You know we haven't done it in a hospital," he said rubbing my leg.

"Mr. Sutton, sit down and relax yourself," I said.

"Let me just get a quickie in before the doctor comes," he begged.

"You are such a freak," I said jabbing him in his chest. "Get away from me."

"You weren't saying that last night," he said.

Just then the door slowly swung open and the doctor walked in.

Dr. Rainer was a middle-aged woman. I felt more comfortable with a female checking me out. She was very nice and informative. She gave me my annual exam and then drew some blood and urine. After about thirty minutes of waiting she returned. She wrote a few things down on her clipboard as we all sat in silence.

"Let me be the first to congratulate you Mommy and Daddy," she finally said. She then did an ultrasound so we could see the baby.

We both sat starring at the small bean like figure in the screen in pure amazement. I was pregnant. He wanted to tell everyone, but I was a little hesitant 'cause news like this could travel quickly. And with us not being married and him being famous it was like asking to be put on the front page of a gossip column. Of course I told Dana and the people at my job. I wanted to wait and surprise my mom. We would be traveling back to Memphis for Dana and Vince's wedding anyway. She wanted to have the wedding there so family could attend. Tone told his entire team and they were all thrilled. A baby can really change your outlook on life.

Chapter 23

Time seemed to fly by. I was now five months pregnant, and had moved in with Tone. Although I had a little pug belly, I still made sure I was dressed to impress everyday at work. My boss always complimented me on that. That Monday, I was given a new project at work. It would show mothers how to be trendy during pregnancy. I wrote articles on what to wear and not to wear. The photographer told me about a new maternity boutique in downtown that was owned by her cousin.

My boss thought it would be great to show off the new clothes in our magazine so that way we would bring business to the boutique and boost ratings for Urban Trends. I was the personal model for the outfits during my pregnancy. She thought that would be a great idea because there is a lot of young business women who were pregnant and wanted to look good at work. Tone was so protective and always watched what I ate. He would jog with me every Saturday morning to make sure I was keeping in shape. He would read to my stomach and rub it every night.

When we found out it was a boy, he went crazy. He decorated the nursery with football stuff and wanted him to be a junior, which was okay with me. He had our son's future planned already. Over breakfast, we argued over whether he would be a football or basketball player. I knew he would make a great father, but there was always this little thing in the back of my head.

That night on the dock, I had unprotected sex with Robert. And that same night, I had sex with Tone. I pushed those thoughts to the back of my head. Besides, in my heart I knew this was Tone's baby. He had been there from the beginning and no matter what he would love this child like his own. I prayed about it and decided to never say anything or bring it up. Besides I had other things to do.

Dana's wedding was in a few weeks. We were running around like chickens with our heads cut off. Dana had the Cadre Building rented out to have the wedding and the reception. I made Dana promise not to tell my mom I was pregnant or engaged. I wanted to double surprise her. Tone wasn't able to come 'cause they had a game that Sunday, but he sent his love.

Dana and I booked an early morning flight to Memphis. At the ATL airport Tone was sad to see me leave. This would be our first time apart for a while since we got back together. Even when he went on out of town trips with the team, he would call daily to see if I was alright.

"You promise to eat right," he asked getting down on one knee to kiss my belly.

"Yes," I said as Junior kicked back against his hand.

"See, I told you he'd be a football player," he said smiling.

Dana helped me carry my bags onto the carrier. The flight was only forty-five minutes. We landed, and our rental car was waiting for us at the port. We took a tour ride around town. I hadn't been in Memphis for a while, and I wanted to see the sites. We drove down the winding rode to my mom's house. It was fall and I loved driving to her house. All the trees had leaves of numerous colors.

The scenery inspired me to write. I pulled out my pad and wrote about the changing of the seasons.

"The writer's at work again," Dana asked, looking over at me.

She knew how passionate I was about writing.

"Yeah, just a little something," I said.

I felt a lump in my throat when we pulled up in my mom's driveway. I guess the baby could feel it too 'cause he was kicking like a wild horse. I patted him to calm him down as I got out and grabbed my bags. I had Dana stand in front of me at the door.

My mom opened the door and hugged Dana. She told her how much she missed her. She looked her up and down surprised at how much she changed since the last time she'd seen her.

"Girl, look at you. You look beautiful. Let me see that rock. It's gorgeous," she said embracing Dana again. "Sharon will be stopping by later tonight."

I cleared my throat so they could recognize I was still standing there.

"Don't let me interrupt this precious moment, but I'm getting tired of standing here in the doorway. It is a little chilly. You know it is fall," I said, sarcastically.

Dana walked on in and my mom dropped her mouth on the floor when she saw me. I had made a few changes since she last saw me. She never saw my hair cut off that short or this reddish color. I had it trimmed right before the flight so I wouldn't have to bother with it during the wedding. And not to mention I was pregnant. I was still my regular shape, but I had a pug belly. I showed her my hand and in my best Shug Avery voice from 'The Color Purple', I said "I's getting married too." We all laughed at my impression.

She was happy to see the ring, but not as glad to see the belly. She wanted me to be married first. I told her I was back with Tone, and she was happy about that 'cause she felt I was truly in love with him. I told her about him a while ago, and she told me if I ever met up with him again to make things right. I guess she figured I made things right by looking at me.

She cried as she welcomed me into her house. Her little girl was having a baby, and she was now a grandma.

"Have you ever seen such a good looking grandmother in your life," she said modeling.

"I'm sorry for keeping it a secret, but I wanted to tell you face-to-face."

"I understand," she said.

We sat down and looked through a catalog to pick out what dishes and centerpieces we would use at the reception. We laughed and talked about old times as we sat in the kitchen eating vegetable soup. My mom always knew how to make the home feel so festive during the holidays. Tone and I had already planned to come down and spend Christmas with her. I wanted to be with her and help her cook and decorate the house. It would be like old times when I use to help her with the tree when I was younger.

When Sharon showed up, the mood changed. Sharon hugged Dana with the fakest hug I'd ever seen. She didn't even use both hands. You could tell they weren't that close anymore, but nobody was to blame, but herself, and she knew it. When Sharon saw my stomach she just sighed. She came over to me and I stopped her before she could even waste her affection on me.

"Who's the daddy," she asked pointing at my stomach.

"The man who gave me this," I said flashing her my hand.

She marveled at each diamond.

"He some kind of drug dealer or something," she asked smirking.

"No, he's a NFL player.

"Well, just making sure you are married before filling the world with children," she said.

"No matter how I go about it, one thing is for sure, I won't put my child second to anyone, not even the father."

I knew that burnt her deep.

"It's getting late. We really should be going," my mom said trying to be the peacemaker.

We all went to David's Bridal to pick out a wedding dress for Dana. After hours of searching, we finally found the right one. It was white and strapless with a long, lacy, white train. She had the shape for it. Her colors were navy blue, pewter, and cream. The wedding would be held in late October. She wanted an outside ceremony and I told her fall would be perfect. The color of the trees would set off her pictures.

We already had her bridesmaids' dresses. We found them in Atlanta, but we could never find the gown that stood out to her. We went from store-to-store looking for the matching shoes. We finally ended up going in K's Shoe Shop. It wasn't that many people in the store and I didn't see an attendant anywhere. We sat and waited on a bench for someone to help us.

I didn't even have to turn around to see his face. When I heard the mellow voice I knew it was Kevin. He asked did we need any help. Dana told him her size and told him what she was looking for. He left then after a few minutes he came back with a few boxes of different heels for her to try on. When he walked around to the front of the sitting area he nearly stumbled when he saw me. He gave Dana the pumps and just nodded at me.

"Damn, a head nod is all I get after all we been through," I exclaimed.

He held out his arms toward me and I got up and hugged him.

Junior kicked as if to say get off my mom. He jumped back and looked down at my stomach.

"Kema told me you moved to Atlanta and had gotten engaged to a famous NFL player," Kevin said.

"Yes, that is true. I'm back 'cause Dana, my cousin here, is getting married in a few weeks.

"Congratulations to both of you then," he said going to help another customer that was asking for help.

I figured he was mad because I hadn't spoken to him since after what happened in the parking lot of Club X. He should get over that, I sure had. Dana purchased the heels she liked most and we were off.

The end of October we flew back down to Memphis, and the wedding went as planned. The whole day was perfect. Tone and I flew back to Atlanta the next evening as Vince and Dana set off to Hawaii for their honeymoon. The Christmas season Tone and I went to my mom's house and spent it with her. He knew that meant so much to me. I loved her country log cabin style house.

After the holidays Tone was rarely at home. His team had made it to the playoffs and had a chance of going to the super bowl, which was the upcoming February. The unbelievable had happened. They won every playoff game and were on their way. Due to inclement weather in the prior chosen city, the Super Bowl was going to be held in the city of Atlanta, and as usual, Dana and I were in the skybox cheering them on. It was cold, but the fans still poured out to support the team. Atlanta was playing the world champion LA Rams. After a very rough and close game, Atlanta finally won. We were all celebrating in the locker room when my water broke. I didn't really recognize it from all the champagne they were pouring all over everyone. But when I felt a hard tug in the bottom of my abdomen, I went down to the floor in pain. When I screamed out the room fell silent.

"The baby is coming," Dana screamed, scampering to my aid.

It didn't take the ambulance long to get there. Tone still had on his uniform as he rode with me. He held my hand and comforted me the entire ride. I was rushed into the nearest hospital and into a delivery room.

Everything was happening so fast. Doctors and nurses were running around me like something was wrong. Dana called my mom and told her I was in labor. I talked to my mom until the pain came back and I couldn't talk anymore.

After only two hours of labor and strenuous pushing, Antonio Jr. was brought into this world. The nurses cleaned him up then brought him back in to us. He was a handsome baby. He had the perfect little round head and big, hazel eyes. He was finally here, and I never knew I could love someone so much. I kissed each one of his toes and fingers.

"I told you. My boy came on the same night his dad won the super bowl. My little football player," Tone said.

"Yeah, our little athlete," I said as I kissed Junior's nose.

Tone videoed everything from Junior's first step, to his first words.

He was so attentive to everything. He loved that little boy and it made my heart sink to see them together, running around the house. Everywhere we went, there were cameras taking photos. I would sometimes read the magazines, talking about NFL players and their families. It would make me mad to see them refer to me as a girlfriend instead of a fiancé. We had plans to get married on that upcoming next year in April.

Dana helped me get things situated. We were going to use Vince's backyard for the actual wedding ceremony. It was huge and he had magnolia trees that gave off a romantic feel. My dress hung in Dana's closet. It was a white gown with diamonds encrusted all over like a Cinderella gown. I felt like a princess the first time I put it on and knew I wanted to purchase it. Tone had a white tux that I knew he would look great in it. Our dreams were finally coming true.

# SECTION 9

The Truth Hurts

Chapter 24

It was a sunny, breezy Monday morning. I got Jr. ready for daycare before I dressed and rushed downstairs to fix him breakfast. In thirty minutes we were at Kiddie Palace and I was on my knees kissing him goodbye and off to work.

I had two meetings that morning and wasn't looking forward to any of them. I was deep in presentation in my second conference after lunch when the receptionist ran in and whispered to me that there had been a horrible accident involving a daycare van and a pickup truck. I knew that Jr.'s class was going to the Zoo that morning, but never did I think something would go wrong. I excused myself and rushed to my office and called the Kiddie Palace center to find out what happened.

"May I speak with Sheila," my son's teacher," I asked.

"This is she. Oh Ms. Smith, I'm so sorry," she said crying.

"What is it? What happened?"

"One of the vans was returning from the zoo when the accident happened. They were merging onto the expressway when a pickup truck swerved out of control and slammed into them. They were hit from the side and thrown over the embankment. The kids had to be pried from the vehicle because it landed upside down," she said.

"Where is my son now," I asked, panicking.

"They were rushed of to Watercress Hospital," she replied.

Before she could say anything else, I hung up and grabbed my keys and was on my way down the elevators to my car. I prayed that my little man was okay. I called Tone on his cell, but got his voicemail. I figured he was still in practice for upcoming the NFL Pro Bowl game. I called and left a message on Dana's phone, letting her know where I was just in case she saw Tone first. I screeched in the small parking lot and ran to the emergency room. It was total chaos everywhere. Nurses were running back and forth while parents were yelling trying to find out if their children were alright.

"I need to see my son. His name is Antonio Sutton Jr.," I rambled.

The old frail lady that smelt of mothballs sitting behind the desk just eye balled me, sneeringly.

"Darling, you're gonna have to calm down. I can't understand what you are saying," she said.

I took a deep breath and said it over again.

"I'm sure he is here, but the nurses have been rushing so they haven't had the time to get all the children's paperwork up to me to get processed into the computer. Why don't you fill out these papers since you're here? Take a seat over there and once you're done bring the documents back to me and I'll try to go and find out where he has been placed," she said, laying the board and papers on the countertop.

A professional person would have taken the clipboard and sat down and filled them out, but the ghetto part of me came out instead. I threw the items back at her.

"Look granny, I don't know what kind of hospital y'all running here, but I want to see my son right now. There was a terrible accident, and I don't know if he is dead or alive and you are giving me something to fill out. What the hell is wrong with you? I'll fill the papers out once I know he's okay," I shouted.

I was getting nervous hearing buzzers and machines beeping loudly as they constantly wheeled bloody children in on stretchers.

"Well, young lady, I can't help you if you gonna take that kind of attitude. You will have to wait for a nurse to call back the parents of the child," she said.

"That won't be necessary. I'm going back there myself," I said as I walked past her desk.

She yelled out for security as I walked through the double doors. She could call the army I didn't care. There was no way I was leaving without seeing my baby. There were only fourteen rooms in the small hallway and I peeked in each one. In the last one, I saw my son laying flat on his back in the bed. They had ripped his little shirt off and they were trying to stop the blood from pouring out of his side. I fell to the floor crying and screaming at the site of it all. A young intern doctor came and helped me to my feet.

"Are you Mrs. Smith," he asked.

"Yes," I said sobbing.

"I'm sorry you had to see him like this. What happened is your son was in a wreck. The force of the truck hitting the van on the side threw him and his car seat through a side window. The seat belt in the car seat saved his life. Long pieces of metal cut him deep and caused damage to one of his kidneys. He is losing a lot of blood and we will have to do a transfusion. We will also have to do surgery to remove that bad kidney before it gets worse," he said, trying to comfort me.

The thought of it made me cringe. I sat down in the hall on the floor weeping to myself. A nurse cane and got me to begin the procedure to draw blood. Due to me being highly anemic from my low iron deficiency they couldn't use my blood. They wanted me to call his father and have him come in to give blood. I called Robert and Tone and let each of them know they were needed at the hospital right away. I hoped they would arrive at different times so I wouldn't have to go through this today, but that didn't happen. Dana had already showed up and was consoling me when they both walked in. The nurse let us use an empty room to discuss matters. I sat them both down although they were looking puzzled. I slowly walked over to Robert and looked him straight in the eye. It was finally time to put it all out there.

"Robert, I should have told you sooner, but I just didn't feel it was necessary. Do you remember that night at Vince's house when I stormed out in the rain and you met me on the dock," I asked.

"Yeah, what about it? You ain't got AIDs or nothing do you," Robert asked, frowning.

"No. We had sex with no protection then the same night Tone showed up at my door and I had sex with him also. I got pregnant, but I honestly thought it was Tone's, but there was always that thought in my mind that it may not be. They calculated back my conception date to that week."

"I can't believe this shit," Tone said, storming over to the window.

"What is this got to do with me," Robert asked.

"Jr. was hurt in an accident, and needs blood. I have low iron and can't give mines. This is the only way to help him and find out who the daddy is all at once," I said.

Talk about killing two birds with one stone. Robert was shocked, but he said he would do whatever to find out if Jr. was really his or not. I turned to Tone and he was red in the face with anger. I understood why. I had kept secrets from him.

"I'm outta here," Tone said grabbing his coat.

"Tone, please wait. I know you're upset, but this is hard for me to. Believe me when I say I never meant for things to go down like this. Don't do it for me do it for Jr.," I begged.

He sat back down. Tone loved that boy and would do anything for him. But now to find out that he may not be his crumbled his world. The nurse came in and took blood samples and saliva from both of them. After about a half hour later, she returned and told me to come out in the hall. She whispered in my ear that Mr. Sutton wasn't the father. I almost was breathless. Now I had to break the news and tell him. Robert was a perfect match. I went back into the room and told Robert the news then the nurse rushed him off to give more blood.

Dana, Tone, and I sat in silence. Tone glared at me.

"You fucking liar. Why didn't you tell me from the beginning? I could have understood and been prepared. You are no better than those hoes trying to scam and get money in the streets," he shouted.

It hurt me to hear him say that. That wasn't me, and he knew it. I loved him and didn't tend for things to go this way. What was done was done and couldn't be changed. I got up and rubbed the back of his head.

"We can get past this and move on with our future. You know how much I care for you. I know you feel the same way," I said.

He pushed my arms away from his face.

"Our future, or you and Robert's? Do you think I can be with you or even look at you after what just happened?"

He didn't even let me answer. He grabbed his jacket and walked out. My heart sank deep in my chest. I sat silently next to Dana as she rubbed my hand. Robert returned in the room saying that he had given blood for Jr. He sat next to me and rubbed my arm. He seemed to be a gentleman about the whole situation.

"It's okay Niyah. I'm not mad at you. You didn't know. I want to be a part of my child's life now that I know he's mines," Robert said.

I knew that it would be hard 'cause Jr. knew Tone as daddy. Now he would have to start all over with Robert. The nurse came and told me Jr. was on his way to surgery and if I wanted to see him I could do so. I rushed to his side as he mumbled out for me. I reassured him I was there and told him I loved him and would be waiting when he got out. When he asked about his dad, I got nervous. I was upset with Tone for leaving like he did, but I understood why he had to do so. He was mad and had to blow off some steam. I held Jr.'s hand and kissed his head as they rolled him off to surgery. He was in surgery for hours. I called my mom and told her what happened and she wanted to fly in. I assured her everything was under control. I didn't want to inconvenience her in any way. I knew Dana had things to do at home, so I told her it was alright to go and that I would call her later.

"Um. I hate to leave out like this, but I have prior engagements," Robert said.

"What," I asked. I thought you were going to check on Jr. when he comes out of surgery."

"I have a date later tonight. This stuff did pop up at the last minute."

I could have argued with him, but there was no way I would force him to stick around for a son he never knew about. He was my son and my responsibility and mines alone. I was prepared to sit there all day if I had to.

"Go on. Do what you please," I shouted.

"I'll call you later to see how things turned out," he said.

"Don't fucking bother you asshole," I yelled. "Just go."

It started to rain, and was beginning to get dark.

A nurse popped in and checked on me every few minutes to see if I needed anything. I called Tone and left a message, but he never returned my call. After four hours of surgery, the doctor came back in to me with bad news. The blood transfusion went well, but when they were in the process of removing the damaged kidney and his little heart just couldn't take it. I didn't cry or say a word. I just stared at this man telling me these horrible things. I wouldn't be able to hold my baby again or hear his sweet little, raspy voice saying Mommy. I missed him already and wanted him near to hold.

You never know true love until you lose it. I felt empty and heartless like a numb soul. All I could do was sit and weep on the inside. The nurse let me go in and hug Jr. one last time. I whispered in his ear that he would always be in my heart. The nurse asked if I wanted them to call anyone, and I told her no 'cause I didn't have anyone. As I walked slowly down the hall I walked past a few other weeping parents and knew how they felt.

There were newscasters taking reports in the main lobby. They were covering the story of the daycare accident. One of the reporters came up to me to get a story. I told her everything. She asked about the two famous football players she saw me with, but I brushed her off, and left. No way was I getting myself into the mess of explaining it to her.

I drove home and sat in my driveway trying to recollect myself. I called Dana and left a message on her phone about Jr. passing. I called my mom and told her, and it took me a while to get her off the phone crying.

Although I shouldn't have, I went to work the next day. I had my receptionist call my lawyer and set up an appointment after lunch. A few minutes later the receptionist buzzed me saying I had a visitor. I had her direct them to my office. It was Dana. She came to have lunch with me. She wanted to make sure I was fine 'cause she had been calling my cell, and I wasn't answering. She had a feeling I was at work. I was in a quiet, nonchalant mood. Dana helped me work out Jr.'s funeral arrangements. I hadn't heard from Tone, and he didn't come home the night before. I left a message on Robert's phone and he never called back. I figured his date was more important.

Losing my son opened a new chapter on life for me. As Dana and I ate the Italian food, the receptionist ran in with the local newspaper. There I was looking a hot mess on the front page. And the story underneath my dreadful picture was even worse. That bitch of a reporter had twisted all my words around. She talked about the wreck and the children that died. I told her about Jr.'s ailments, and she put them in as well. I guess she talked to one of the staff members 'cause they also put in that I didn't even know who the father was. She elaborated on how I brought in two famous Atlanta NFL football players to take blood tests and none of them were the fathers. The following paragraphs went on to verbally bash me. I felt myself becoming enraged.

Just wait 'til I spoke with my lawyer. They would not get away with bad-mouthing me like that. For years I had written articles about people. Never had I seen one on me. Everyone was talking about it around the office. This could ruin me for sure. Dana said that Vince and all his friends were talking about me badly in practice. Everyone thought Jr. was Tone's baby. Now that it was out that he wasn't, I was a whore in everyone's eyes. Dana said she cleared it up all for me though. I didn't care. My mind was set on my son. He was buried that following Saturday morning. Dana held my hand as they lowered my son into the ground. Sharon and my mom flew in to support me. We all threw blue and white roses onto his little coffin. It shocked me when Tone came and threw in a small football and Jr.'s favorite jersey. He was crying and I could feel his pain. We caught eye contact a few times, but he never held a long gaze with me. After the funeral, I had Vince and a few of his friends help me pack up my things out of Tone's house. I found me a little pint house near work.

After a few court appearances, the driver of the truck that hit the daycare van was convicted on drunk driving and vehicular homicide charges.

Chapter 25

Over the next few months my life changed. I didn't go to any of the parties that Dana or Vince threw. I didn't attend any games or talk to Robert or Tone. No longer would I force anyone to be in my life that didn't honestly want to be there. I was tired of going through the ups and downs of love. I promised myself to never let my heart take over again. It was too painful in the long run.

The wedding was definitely off. I returned the dress and got my money back. I isolated myself from everyone and dove into my work. I was sitting in my living room writing a poem on life when I looked down and saw Tone's ring was still on my hand. I needed to return it to him so I could finally move on.

I knew the team did exercises daily at the stadium. I sat out in the parking lot for about an hour and when nobody came out I went inside to find Tone. I never realized how huge the place was. I walked slow and looked around the arena. I saw the guys doing sprints on the field. I slipped up to Coach Matthews and asked if it was possible if I spoke with Tone. He hugged me and shared his condolences.

"Tone, get over here," Coach yelled out.

Tone just looked over, and then kept on tossing the ball.

I burst out in tears and ran up to the exit door. Tone caught up with me by the time I got to the door. I didn't want to look at him or say a word to him. I just pulled the ring off of my finger and handed it to him.

"Why you giving this back? I gave it to you. You can keep it. I don't have a need for it anymore."

"I can't. It brings back too many memories that I don't need anymore," I said.

"Fine, but don't think I'm forgiving you. Its gonna take some time. You really hurt and embarrassed me. Do you even know how it feels to be humiliated like that?"

"Tone I'm not asking you for forgiveness. I'm trying to get closure on this whole situation. I believe things happen for a reason. I won't call or come around here again so don't worry."

I then turned and walked out of the door. I didn't give him a chance to say anything. As I was pulling off in the parking lot I saw him come to the exit door as I sped off. Later that night he called me a few times, but I didn't answer.

I just didn't feel the same about residing in Atlanta anymore. It was mid spring and I wanted to move back to Memphis. This fast paced life brought me nothing but problems. I called my mom and we had a long conversation about me coming back. She told me to do whatever I felt was right for me. I still didn't know what to do. The next day, I got a phone call from a very special person that I missed. Ariel called and told me she had dumped that zero and was finally getting her life back together. Hearing from her made up my mind. I was going to go back to Memphis no doubt.

The next day at work I went on the web and looked up current jobs in Memphis. It didn't take long before landed an interview with the Memphis Flyer. A few days later, they called and offered me a job. I hadn't found a place to stay yet, but Ariel was renting a three-bedroom house and said it was cool for me to live with her for a while. I turned in my notice at my current job and was on my way. I didn't even tell Dana I was leaving. I had the moving company move my things into a storage facility.

My mom was happy to see me. I spent the first weekend at her house. I needed her to console me and let me know everything would be alright. I always missed that in life. I never really had a solid person I could go to and lay my heart out to. I had come so far. So many things good and bad had happened to me over the years. I had let so many things and people control my life. But now I was starting over. I would set goals and aspirations for myself that I would reach no matter what.

It didn't take long for Dana to contact my mother. She hadn't heard from me and was wondering what had happened. When my mom told her I had moved back to Memphis, Dana got upset. She thought it was something she did. I told my mom it was alright to give her my cell number. When Dana called I reassured her it was all my idea. Too much went on in the ATL. I wanted to be around people who actually cared about me. I wanted to get back into the grove of things. Living with Ariel was hard, but I made it work. She was messy and the kids would get on my nerves from time-to-time, but it was home. I had even hooked back up with Kema. She finally talked me into going clubbing again.

I knew I said I wouldn't, but I called Darren back up. I needed someone to talk to and show me affection. I made sure this time we kept it strictly a booty-call thing. I never spent the night or let him spend the night. I didn't want to get wrapped up in old feelings again. I would be turning twenty-seven later this year, and it was time to lay my life out and follow some straight paths.

I was shocked to see that Ariel actually kept her word. She never called or invited Frank over. He would meet her over his mother's house and pick up the kids. She was dating a new guy, Reginald. When they made up their minds to move in together, I knew it was time to get my own place. I didn't know of anywhere else, but Darren's place. But instead of living with him, I got my own townhouse in his complex. He was so happy. I assured him I wasn't going down that road with him again. Darren was beginning to annoy the hell out of me. He would call me all hours of the night and sometimes tap at my window if I didn't answer. I held back sexually with him thinking that would make him leave me alone, but it didn't work. We went from having sex every other day to having sex like maybe twice a week. But I guess as long as he could be with me, he was cool with whatever. I wanted something different, but I was afraid to go out and try something new. I had endured so much and didn't want to get hurt again.

Kema had been trying to get me out with her all week. I was busy, but I finally gave in to shut her up. She called me on my cell and told me that I'd better wear something cute and sexy 'cause we were going out to have a ball no matter what. I took a warm shower and laid a few outfits out on my bed. I didn't want all eyes on me, so I wasn't going to wear anything revealing. It was hot outside so I couldn't cover up much. I didn't want to be sweating like a pig on the dance floor. I decided on a tan and turquoise Oriental print sundress. I put on a small diamond solitaire necklace and some matching earrings to enhance my neck and short hair. I dabbed some perfume on my wrist and shoulders. I was sitting down, painting my toenails with some gold polish when the doorbell rang. I slipped on my tan opened-toed sandals and answered it. It was Kema and she whistled at me. I turned around to model for her.

She offered to drive, but I knew that would be a horrible idea. If I ever wanted to leave early she would be lagging around trying to keep me there. So I told her I would follow her instead. She didn't see why, but she went along with it. She hopped in her car as I walked in the garage. When Jr. was born I bought a Yukon. I wanted to make sure I had enough room for his things. And as a gift Tone had bought me a burnt orange drop-top, Infiniti Q60 Coupe. I decided to drive it instead of the truck.

Twenty minutes later we pulled up to Club X. It was the same way as I remembered. We sat at the bar, sipping drinks. I knew I should have left when I saw Sandra and Jovan stroll through the door hand-in-hand. Kema waved for Jovan to come and join us. He hugged me as I gave the evil eye to Sandra over his back. Kema had told me they were back together. I told Kema the story between Sandra and me, but she felt that because that was years ago everything was squashed. There was no way I was going to act as if nothing happened. I didn't back stab Sandra. She did it to me.

I was a grown woman with no time for games and fake people in my life. I grabbed my purse and walked toward the door. Kema rushed up behind me and begged me to at least sit and have a few drinks with them. She pointed at a booth in the far corner that Sandra was seated at. I let her lead the way as I followed slowly behind her. Sandra and Jovan were whispering amongst themselves when we walked up. The table fell silent when I sat down. I didn't care 'cause I wouldn't be there long. The waitress came over, and we ordered some wings. I ordered a cranberry and vodka to sip on. I felt a tap on my shoulder. I turned around and saw it was Terry.

"I thought that was you," he said.

I didn't know if I was happy or upset with seeing him. I got up and hugged him. He hadn't aged much and he still looked good as hell. He stepped back and looked at me. I had gotten a little taller. He never saw me with short hair, but he said it brought out my eyes. He told me my body was still banging as usual.

He had on a cream colored linen outfit with sandals. He still had his Gerald Levert facial hair thing going on. We walked over to the bar and sat down to talk privately. I wanted to go somewhere quiet so we could really talk. I had a lot of questions to be answered. He was acting as if nothing had happened. He was telling me about his new music studio he had opened. I glanced at his ring finger and nothing was there. I just figured when I left that he would go back to Charlotte. But then I thought he hid his ring when he was around me and he could have taken it off. Maybe he was trying to take a woman home tonight. The way I was feeling that woman could just be me.

As we chatted I thought back on those steamy nights we would make love all over the house. I wanted to feel that way again. I didn't know seeing him would bring back memories good and bad. I never talked to or heard from him since the day Dora came and got me from Lena's house. I sat there gazing in his eyes as he went on with his story.

He bought me a few more drinks as we chatted some more. We danced for hours and my feet were killing me. He draped his arms

164

around my waist and let his hands rest on my butt. I wrapped my arms around his neck and rested my head on his chest. I could hear his heart beat and wondered what he was thinking. He then mumbled my name. I met his gaze, and he bent down and whispered in my ear that he missed me. An hour later, I was pulling up in the parking spot next to him at his apartments. I was shocked that he still lived in the same complex we had together. The place still looked the same. We walked hand and hand up to the stairs. A lump came up in my throat as we rounded the base of the steps. Charlotte had stabbed me on the same stairwell. I froze in place as he stepped on up ahead of me. The whole mental scene came back to me, and I began to tremble. He came back down to me to see what the problem was. I screamed out to let my hand go and I ran back to my car. As I fumbled with the keys he caught up with me. After a few tries I finally got the door open. He caught the edge of the door before I could close it.

"What's wrong," he asked.

"I can't go up there," I said.

There were too many memories that I wasn't ready to encounter again.

"Why don't I go with you to your place then?"

"I'm sorry. I just can't go through with this," I said.

I got out of the car and embraced him. He hugged me back as if he knew it was the end. He kissed me on my forehead and then turned and walked away. I drove home in silence thinking about what could have happened. I needed someone to talk to. There were a lot of things going through my head that I needed to get out. I called Kema on her cell, but she didn't answer. I remembered she said they were going to chill at Jovan and Sandra's house after the club, so I called him up. He answered on the second ring. He had a raspy voice, so I knew he was either drunk or sleep. I glanced at the clock and it was a little past three.

"I apologize for calling so late. Is Kema there," I asked.

"Kema and Sandra went on to another club. I was tired and came home. Sandra said she was going to spend the night over Kema's," he replied.

I guess he could hear the displeasure in my voice.

"You need something," he asked concerned.

"Yeah, a shoulder to cry on," I replied, softly.

"Well, if I hear from Kema I'll let her know you called."

"Thanks," I said before hanging up.

I took me a hot shower and laid down, but I couldn't fall asleep. I tossed for a few minutes, and then looked at the clock and it was going on four. I wanted to be comforted. I got up and slipped on my black stilettos and put on my light black trench coat. I walked down to Darren's complex. I saw his car and another car parked in his two parking spots. I didn't recognize the car, so I walked up anyway. All his lights were out, so I crept around to the back patio. I took his balcony steps up to his room window. His bedroom light was off. As I got near his window to tap on it, I could hear the moans and whispers of a woman. I peeked through the edge of the blinds and could see two silhouettes in his bed. I sat on his balcony for a few moments, and then decided to take a ride. I got in my car and drove around for a while. I couldn't go back home alone. I made a left on Ridgeway and headed toward Jovan's house. I remembered Kema telling me the address earlier that night. I pulled up to his condo. I parked in the empty spot next to his car, which I figured was Sandra's. It was quiet outside. All you could hear was the clacking of my heels against the pavement. I could hear loud jazz music coming from the living room. The blinds were partially opened, so I climbed into the flower garden and peeked in. He was lying on the couch sipping wine from a goblet. I stood there for a few seconds to make sure he was alone. It might have been the alcohol I had consumed earlier, but Jovan was looking good to me. I softly tapped at the window and watched his reaction. He put down his glass and jumped up quickly. He came over to the window and pulled back the blinds. When he saw it was me, he hurried me around to the front. He opened the door and asked me to come in. He offered to take my coat, but I refused. I was naked under there and didn't want him to think I came over to seduce him. He got me a dry towel, and I blotted my hair and face.

"You want something to drink," he asked.

"No, I'm good," I replied.

He sat back down and sipped some more of his red wine. He cut the music down to a low whisper. They had a fake fireplace with fake logs burning behind the couch. I went over to the fireplace and looked at the pictures. I always knew Sandra and he were meant to be. They looked so happy together in the photos. It was so quiet you could feel the tension in the room.

"I'm sorry you wasted a ride over here. I thought I told you Sandra and Kema weren't coming home," he said.

"I know. I just needed to get out and get some fresh air."

166

I could tell he wanted to be alone, so I walked over to the door with him slowly following behind me.

"Good night Jovan," I said.

He sipped some more of his wine from his cup and replied to me the same. We stood there gawking at each other.

"You know what? I could use a drink," I said taking the goblet from his hand and drinking the remaining portion of it.

He looked a little startled.

"I had a rough night and that hit the spot. I'm gonna head out. Do you mind if I get a hug before I go? I really could use one," I said.

He gave me a one armed embrace.

"Not like that. I want the kind you give to Sandra."

He smiled a coy smile and pulled me closer, cradling me softly.

I rested my head on his shoulder, and I could hear him sniff my hair. He moaned out loud as his arms went lower down my back. I could feel his penis swelling through his lounging pants. I knew he was turned on, and it was up to me to make the move to let him know I wanted him as well. I pulled away from him and gave him an angry glare. He apologized numerous times, and I smiled at him. He was so nervous like we were school kids again. I unbuckled my coat and let it fall to the floor. A look of astonishment crept across his face. He locked the deadbolt lock on the door and guided me back over to the couch.

"You don't know how long I wanted to see you like this," he whispered.

"Don't talk. I want you to fuck me," I demanded.

I threw him down on the sofa and pulled off his house shoes. I took off his pants as he pulled his shirt over his head. I kissed him slowly from his navel back up to his chin. I sucked and nibbled on his neck as he moaned out in pleasure. When I met his mouth he turned me over quickly. He got up and picked me up and carried me upstairs to his bedroom. He kicked the door close and threw me onto the bed. He got down on his knees and pulled me to the foot of the bed. He put my left leg over his shoulder and my right leg slightly out to the side.

"I've dreamed of tasting your body Niyah."

He took two fingers and spread my vagina lips apart and blew softly on my clitoris. He then took his tongue and licked my clit softly. Once he tasted my sweet love juices he went to town. He sucked like he was drinking out of a straw, which made me cum quick. He then spread my legs out as far as they could go and licked rapidly up and down 'til I climaxed again. By the time he was tongue fucking me I had cum three times and my body was twitching. He devoured all my juices 'til I was dry. He then stood up and rubbed the head of his penis on my vagina lips. I was getting turned on again. I wanted to be on top and he was all for it. He lay across the bed and retrieved a condom from the nightstand. He was moaning and shouting loudly. I had to put one of my breasts in his mouth to shut him up. I didn't want the neighbors to hear 'cause they would know that wasn't Sandra's car parked outside.

I was rough with him, and he hung on for dear life to my hips as each stroke brought us closer to ecstasy. I turned around and rode him backwards. With each plunge downward on his penis he yelled out my name. We came in unison and I collapsed forward on the bed. As I tried to regroup myself he got up and was sliding his penis, back in me from behind. I lay there and let him do all the work.

A short while later, we lay across the bed exhausted. He had really worn me out. I was soaked in our juices and I wanted to wash up. After I showered and put my coat back on, he walked me to my car. He kissed me on my cheek and I was off.

The sun had risen. I looked at my cell and it was almost seven. As I turned my burnt orange Infiniti coupe right out onto Ridgeway, I saw Sandra turn in. I couldn't have timed it more perfectly. Thank goodness I had tinted windows or she would have seen me. I knew Jovan would keep a secret, so I wasn't worried.

Chapter 26

I drove to IHOP and ordered two pancake and turkey sausage plates to go. I pulled up to Darren's house and his company was gone. I knocked on his door and one of his old friends answered. I asked if Darren was there, and he walked me over to the couch. Darren was lying under a huge blanket. He looked like hell. There was a half-drunken glass of orange juice and Kleenexes all over the coffee table. He was fast asleep. I now knew that wasn't him in his room last night. I sat down on the floor next to the couch and ate my breakfast. I gave the other plate to his friend. Darren woke up coughing and was happy to see me sitting there.

"I just came by to check on you since I hadn't heard from you in a while," I said.

He leaned down and kissed the top of my head.

"I came by last night, but I didn't bother you. I thought you had company."

"Naw, that was Ron. He had a girl over and they kept me up most of the night."

He sat on the floor and leaned his head in my lap. I still enjoyed talking to him and hanging out with him. I think it was because he was dependable. A woman loves when she can have a man drop what he is doing just to come and see what she needs. We weren't dating, but to the outside eye, we were. We went out to eat quite a bit. He would shower me with gifts, and we'd stay up all night on some nights talking on the phone. It wasn't all about sex. I didn't want to lead him on or lose him. I always made him think we were working on getting to know each other again. I told him that once we worked things out we would get back together.

Darren began sneezing profusely.

"I'll go and you call me when you're feeling better," I said.

"I'm fine. I'm going upstairs to take a shower. Can I leave with you? If you don't mind," he asked.

"It's cool I guess."

I really wanted a day of peace and quiet, but I guess it would be okay to have company.

He ran upstairs to get dressed.

We spent the entire day together. We went to lunch at Bonefish grill and caught an afternoon matinee movie. We were both in my kitchen preparing baked chicken breast, steamed veggies, and rice later that evening when the phone rang. I almost didn't hear it over us laughing and the music playing on my stereo. I answered the phone, but the person on the other end was whispering. I stepped into the hall to hear them better. It was Jovan. He wanted to know when he could taste me again. I hung up in his face. I didn't need this shit right now. Didn't he understand it was just a one nightstand? Men could be so stupid. Sandra was going to find out something happened if he didn't slow his roll.

When I returned to the kitchen Darren had a sly smile on his face.

"Warn your niggas not to call when I'm over," he said.

I played it off as a wrong number.

He set the table as I put the finishing touches on dinner. It was cool outside so we decided to relax out there for a bit. We sat on my lawn furniture on the balcony. I could smell the rain in the air. We sat close to each other under a fleece blanket. I got lost in his intoxicating body aroma. I leaned my head into his chest and dozed off. The loud crashing of thunder woke us up. We quickly gathered our wineglasses, pillows, and blankets and ran inside. We ended the night on a perfect note. I had to go to work in the morning, so he left early. He kissed me on the back of my hand and ran to his place in the rain.

I slipped on my nightclothes and got in bed. I had a big day ahead of me in the morning. I was given the opportunity to start a new article in the local paper. It would be a small section about young urban life in the metro city. I hoped people would be drawn to it, and make it popular.

Right when I was about to doze off my phone rang again. I readied myself to curse Jovan out, but it was Kema.

"I've been looking for you all night girl," I said.

"Jovan told me this morning. What's up?"

"Nothing much," I said lying.

I was glad Jovan didn't tell her about me stopping by.

Who was that fine ass guy you left the club with?"

"An old friend. You are so nosy," I said.

"I'm sure he was. But anyway, I called to tell you what happened. Sandra called me crying not too long ago. She said she returned home early this morning and Jovan was lying across the bed naked. When she got in bed to join him he pushed her away and told her he was too tired to do anything. She even tried sucking his dick and still nothing, not even a flinch. She was so upset that she went downstairs to sleep on the couch and that was when she found a wine goblet. It was on the coffee table with lipstick on it," Kema said.

I could have slapped Jovan. Why in the hell was he laying across the bed naked? I left him with clothes on?

"Sandra's pissed and wants to know who the cheap ass bimbo was, but Jovan isn't saying anything."

"That is so messed up," I said smiling.

*I should have never gone there,* I thought to myself.

Kema had stated that Sandra was staying over at her place. I guess that was why Jovan was calling me.

After work the next evening, I babysat Ariel's kids while she and Reginald went out to eat. Darren had rented some Redbox movies and wanted to watch them with me. I told him I was watching the kids and he offered to come by and keep me company. I felt like a schoolgirl. He looked good in his jeans and black t-shirt. His leather jacket made his shoulders stand out even more. He had gotten his head and facial hair trimmed.

We stood in the doorway smiling at each other. The kids were standing holding on to my leg watching our every move. I introduced him to each of them. I was glad it was comedy movies he rented, so the children would have something to do. We made a pallet on the living room floor and watched movies 'til the kids fell asleep. I was lying on one end of the couch and he was on the other end. I had my feet in his lap, and he was massaging them. He started kissing each of my toes. I tried to make him stop 'cause I didn't want the children to wake up.

He got up and came over to my side. He wrestled me down until I gave in. I checked the little ones, but they were dead asleep. We were getting undressed when I heard Ariel talking outside the door. We rushed and put our clothes back on. I didn't tell her I had hooked back up with Darren or that he was coming over. I knew she would be mad when she saw him. The door creaked and slowly opened, and we jumped back up on the couch. We were sitting in the dark. Reginald cut the light on. Ariel cut her eyes at me. She must have known something was about to go down.

"So running with dogs again I see", she said. "Girl I don't get you sometimes. You are too talented and beautiful for this. He cheated on you, so why are you with him? You need sex that bad I'll have Reginald hook you up with one of his boys. I'm tired of being your shoulder to lean on when you get hurt. You have to be mature and notice a dog when you see one. When are you going to stop being a dummy?"

I glared at her.

Darren got up and walked out. Ariel knew I was upset, and I understood what she was saying, but she was wrong for bringing it up like that. That was something we should have done one on one in private.

Reginald gathered the kids and took them off to bed. Ariel was in the kitchen still ranting on about cheaters when I clicked.

"Will you shut up already? How in the hell are you of all people giving me advice? You dated the king of dogs. He got you knocked up three times. And after each pregnancy he left you high and dry, yet you managed to run right back to him. He beat you and never helped out with the kids. He even gave you a STD. Yet you skipped your way back after you were cured. You gave me a place to stay when I needed that, but don't think you can be my mother, Ariel. That is your problem. If you put half the energy into your own children that you put on these men you pick up you'd be okay. I am head strong, and got a lot going for myself, which is more than I can say for you," I said.

She stood there speechless.

I didn't mean for those things to come out, but she pulled them out of me. I grabbed my purse and jacket and went to the door.

"And another thing, find you another damn babysitter since I'm so dumb", I said as I slammed the door shut behind me.

I got in my car and sped home. She had pissed me off. I hadn't let anyone get under my skin like that since the argument with Sandra. I called Kema on my way home and told her what happened. After I got off the phone with her, I left a message on my mother's phone. She and her new man where on a cruise. She had called me the day before I came home and told me they would be gone for a week. I was so happy she was getting back into the grove of things, but I needed to talk to her. I didn't leave a bad message, I just said I missed her and to call me when she returned.

I pulled up to my complex and saw Darren sitting on the bottom of my steps. He looked so sad. I walked up to him, and he leaned his head face first into my stomach. I rubbed his head and assured him everything was cool.

"I wish I could take it all back. I always hated that saying 'once a cheater always a cheater'. Once and for all I'm gonna prove that saying is false," he said.

The next two months flew by like a breeze. Darren and I were seeing so much of each other. We still hadn't confirmed anything, but we were getting close again. He had given me the key to his place.

That Labor Day weekend, I had planned to take a flight to see Dana in Atlanta. He was sad to see me go, but I missed her and wanted to see her. He dropped me off at the airport. I couldn't do it. I was too nervous. I didn't want those bad memories I buried in the back of my mind about Atlanta to come back. I apologized to the luggage guy who had to retrieve my bags from the plane. The attendant told me that I wouldn't be able to get my money back, but I didn't care. I just knew I couldn't get on that plane. I would call Dana as soon as I got home and tell her a fake story about why I couldn't come.

I called Kema to pick me up 'cause I knew Darren would be upset that I chickened out after I made so many plans. I didn't want her to take me straight home, so I decided to go by her house first. We went and got sub sandwiches and kicked it at her crib. It was getting late so I had her drive me to my house. I hopped in my car 'cause I had some errands to run. I drove to Ariel's house. I wanted to make it right between us. I had stopped by Hallmark and bought the perfect card. It said all the words I couldn't say. She was pulling up with groceries. I blew my horn, so she could see me. I got out and walked up to her. The kids came and hugged me and then they helped Reginald with the bags. She stood there with her hand on her hips as I stared at the ground. I handed her the envelope. She opened it and read it, then grabbed my arms and hugged me. We were both crying. We didn't speak, but we knew what each other was saying. She told me to call her tomorrow and we would do lunch.

I called and ordered some PF Chang's takeout for Darren and I and picked it up on the way to his place. I hadn't called him all day, and I was going to surprise him. I pulled up to his house and there was a car in his other parking spot. I had a key so I opened the door and the entire house was dark.

I went into the kitchen and placed the bags on the countertop. I could hear footsteps running around upstairs.

*At it again old Ron,* I thought to myself.

I poured me some juice in a glass and sat on the couch. I rubbed Darren's feet while he slept.

He had the cover pulled up over his head and was snoring lightly.

I put down my cup and climbed on top of him.

He moaned under his breath as I began to grind a little. He was still sleeping so   I rocked back and forth slowly and felt his penis begin to swell up.

"Why don't you take the sheet down and fuck me," I said seductively. "We can show Ron and his friend how it's really done."

"What," Ron said rising his head from under the blanket.

I quickly jumped off of him, falling to the floor.

Anger enraged my body. I ran up the steps and heard groaning. Darren's door was closed and the light was off. I kicked the door open and caught him face down in some girl's pussy.

"Oh my God," the female said, sitting up.

"What are you doing here," Darren said, jumping up.

"You fucking bastard. You haven't changed a bit. You're still the same low life you were before," I said throwing his keys at him.

"Niyah. Wait a minute," he said scampering to get up.

"Who is she," the young girl asked, covering her breast with her hands.

"Nobody apparently," I replied.

"Baby please," he said grasping at my arm.

"Get your hands off of me. Don't you fucking touch me. I don't want to hear your lies."

I stormed out.

I went back into the kitchen and got my food and drove to Ariel's house.

We sat on her porch as I gave her a run down on what had just taken place.

"I can't believe he did it to me again. I'm such a fool," I shouted.

"I told you so just doesn't seem right at this particular moment," she said.

She held my head as I leaned on her shoulder and cried. She was truly my best friend. Ariel was right although I hated to admit it.

# SECTION 10

## Square One

Chapter 27

Later that night when I left her house, I rode past Darren's place and he and the girl were outside in the driveway. It seemed as if they were arguing. She had her hand in his face. I wanted him to see me as I rode by, so I crept by slowly with the top down. He called me numerous times that night, but I ignored each one. The first thing I did the next morning was get the number changed.

For weeks I had a common routine. I would go to work and then come home. Kema and Ariel both tried to get me out of the house with no prevail. I was tired of men and the bullshit that came along with them. Why couldn't I meet a nice guy? I was a simple girl who didn't ask for much.

After while, Darren started leaving notes on my door. After a few weeks of me not getting back in contact with him he finally stopped.

One afternoon, I was lying on Ariel's couch in my pajamas, eating a bowl of cereal when Reginald came in.

"Damn girl, what happened to you? You look rough. Look, I told one of my boys about you. Hope you aren't upset. Ariel had me give him your number."

I jumped up in anger.

"What? Y'all should have asked me first," I shouted.

Ariel always did what I told her not to do. Why must people feel it is their job to hook you up? I could find a man of my own if I wanted one.

"Tell your friend not to waste his time by calling," I said.

I was going to ring Ariel's neck the next time I saw her.

The following afternoon, I had just gotten out of the shower when the phone rang. I wrapped a towel around me and ran to answer it. I figured it was Kema.

"Hello. May I speak to a Miss Niyah Smith," a deep voice asked in the receiver. I cleared my throat.

"This is she," I replied.

I didn't catch the voice and thought it was a telemarketer.

"Hi, I'm Allen, Reginald's friend," he said.

"Allen, I don't mean to sound rude, but this was a big mistake. Reginald and Ariel are two nosy people who can't keep their noses out of other people's business."

"Reginald does me the same way," he said laughing.

He had a cute laugh and a nice voice, so I decided to chat with him for a while.

We talked about politics and random life issues. He told me he majored in business and marketing at Lemoyne-Owen College, and just recently got hired at AMK Solutions as a Graphic Designer. I also found out he was an only child and very close to his mother and grandmother. His grandma willed her house to him when she died a few years back. We seemed to have a lot of things in common. We laughed and talked 'til three in the morning.

"Why don't you meet me over Ariel's house this afternoon? They invited me to play cards," he said.

"Isn't that odd. I got that same invitation previously from Ariel," I said.

"Well, it's a date then. I gotta get up for work in a few hours, so I'm gonna say goodnight to you Miss Niyah."

"Same to you," I said, hitting end call on my cell phone.

I turned over in bed and thought back on his mellow voice.

I was looking forward to meeting him. Even if we didn't hit it off romantically, I could see us continuing to be friends.

Around lunchtime at work, Ariel called me.

"You still coming by later," she asked.

"Yes. I talked to Allen."

She fell silent.

"Don't worry. You think you slick don't you," I asked laughing.

"Who me," she said innocently.

"Whatever," I said hanging up.

I rushed home and showered and stood in front of my closet deciding what to wear.

*I don't want to look desperate, or like a thot,* I thought to myself.

I decided on a one-piece denim jumper and matching denim peep toe wedges.

I pulled up to Ariel's place around six. When I saw a white Yukon parked in the driveway, I felt butterflies in my stomach. I checked myself in my side view mirror. My hair had grown out over the weeks. I went to my beautician and got it trimmed in a cute auburn colored bob style. I retouched my lipstick, and put on some small silver hoop earrings. Each step closer to the door made my belly hurt even more. Just as I was about to ring the doorbell my cell rang. And Kema's name flashed across the screen.

"Hello, I whispered, so no one would hear me.

"Where are you? And why are you speaking so low? Anyway, what are you doing later tonight? I'm going to Club X again. Why don't you meet me there," she said.

"Is that your second home or something? You're there almost every night. I can't. I have prior engagements. I'll call you later," I said as I hung up.

I took a deep breath and knocked.

The television was blaring and I could hear yelling. When I heard Allen's voice, I panicked. I turned to run back to my car, but Ariel flung the door open.

"I thought I heard you pull up. Come one in," she said with a big grin planted on her face.

I walked in and saw the guys watching a basketball game. I quietly took a seat on a nearby loveseat.

"How are you? Mind if I sit with you," Allen asked.

"No," I said, moving over to make room.

He was about six feet with a peanut butter complexion, and light brown eyes. He had a gleaming white smile and a dimple in his left cheek. He had on a Shaq's Laker jersey and jeans. His head was shaved low, and his mustache was trimmed. He was wearing Avatar cologne, a scent I loved to smell on a man.

"Instead of playing cards, I'd rather watch the game," I said to Ariel.

Philly was my favorite team, and they were playing the Lakers.

We all screamed and hollered as the two teams scored point after point on each other.

"You like pro basketball I see," Allen said.

"Yeah. I've been known to attend a game or two," I bragged.

"Maybe we can go to one together."

"That would be nice. I'd love to," I said, blushing.

I felt comfortable around him.

Later that night, we ended up playing cards. It was girls against boys. Reginald always cheated so they were beating us bad.

"It's getting late. I should be going," I said yawning.

"Thanks for coming over," Reginald said. "Too bad you and Ariel got whooped."    "I wonder how," I said laughing.

I retrieved my purse and walked towards the door.

"I'd better be heading out as well," Allen said grabbing his jacket. "I got an early morning meeting."

He offered to walk me out although I was parked directly behind him. He walked me to my car and held the door open as I slipped in. We didn't say much, but we kept on catching each other's eyes wandering over each others body. He squatted down just inside my driver's door.

"Would it be okay to call you again," he asked.

"Yeah," I replied.

"I enjoyed myself tonight. We should do this again some time."

"I agree," I said starting up my car.

"You have a safe drive home," he said, closing my door.

I let down the top and waved as I pulled out of the driveway.

The next morning, after a conference with the CEO, I had a message on my cell from Allen. He wanted to know if I was available for the night to accompany him to a play. I wasn't doing anything so I called him up.

"Hi, I got your message. And yeah, I'd love to go," I said.

"Cool. I'll pick you up at seven, he said.

I gave him the directions to my place, and then we talked for a few more minutes before hanging up.

I decided on a long, black satin spaghetti strap dress with a matching shawl. I heard from a friend at work that this was an elegant play, and I wanted to look nice. I dabbed on some perfume and slipped on my black heels as I heard the knock at the door.

"Why didn't you blow the horn," I asked. "I would have come on out."

"You don't toot for a true lady," he said extending his arm for mine.

That made me smile to know he saw me in that way.

We had a wonderful time.

Afterwards, we stopped downtown at Flight and ate dinner. We sipped wine over nice conversation. We pulled up to my house around eleven. He walked me to my door to make sure I made it in okay. As we stood in silence on my porch, a chill wind ripped through my body.

"You cold," he asked rubbing my arms.

"A little," I said nodding my head.

"Well, you better go on in before you catch a cold."

I turned and unlocked my door.

"Thanks for a great evening," I said.

"You are welcome. It helps when you have nice company."

A gave him a slight smile and walked inside.

*This guy must be a true gentleman,* I pondered as I leaned against the closed door.

Friday evening, he invited me over to have dinner at his place. He left the directions on my voicemail.

I pulled up to his crib around eight. It was a white brick house that sat on the corner of a cove. It had a huge front yard and beautiful landscaping. The front walkway had small lights leading up to the porch. Under the front windows were small rose bushes. I tried to peep through the chiseled glass on the front door as I rang the doorbell. I couldn't believe he lived here. He opened the door, and I could smell the aroma of food cooking. He guided me down a long hall and down three steps into the kitchen and dining area. He had candles on the table and soft jazz music playing in the background. He had prepared grilled lemon pepper grilled catfish with salad on the side.

Dinner was marvelous. We both loaded the dishwasher and cleared off the table. He then took me on a tour of the house. The living room had black leather furniture and tan Chinese bamboo décor. I told him about my bedroom and how I loved the Oriental look. Two double doors led to an adjoined office in the back. We walked back down an emerald marble hallway to the den. An entertainment center covered an entire wall from floor to ceiling. On it was a huge screen TV and just about every electronic device known to man. There were two plush king-sized recliners facing it. Behind the chairs was a large fireplace. On top of the mantle was a life-size portrait of Shaq. He had autographed photos and posters hung all over the walls.

Between two bay windows was a glass top table with a stereo on it. His CD collection was impressive.

We went upstairs to see the rest of the house. Along the winding stairs were family photos hung perfectly aligned. He had two guestrooms. I was falling in love with the house, and I hadn't even seen his room yet. I was taken aback at how clean and tidy it was. He said his grandmother had it built from the ground up a few years back.

"Did an ex girlfriend help you decorate?"

"No. I hired a professional," he said. "I have her card if you want the number."

"That's okay. I like to think I have a creative eye myself when it comes to interior designing."

His phone began to ring but he didn't flinch or answer it.

"Follow me," he said.

His room was at the opposite end of the hall. He opened the two white doors and I could have passed out. The walls were made of dark cherry wood with matching mini blinds. An oak dresser and Chester occupied one corner. Next to a huge window was a mirror and chair stand. He said it belonged to his grandmother and he just didn't have the heart to throw it out. I assured him that it was beautiful and that he shouldn't get rid of it at all.

We walked around a partition to a king sized sleigh bed which was made up with royal blue cotton sheets and matching comforter.

Abstract art adorned the walls. They ranged in vast shades of blue. His room had a romantic feel to it.

The restroom had wooden panel walls also. On the wall near the door was a tall blue vase with bamboo sticks in it. The towels and accessories matched the colors in his bedroom. The tub was an antique, and stood on four legs. A chiseled glass shower stall sat next to the tub.

I sat on his bed and marveled at the scenery.

"I love this house," I said.

"Thank you," he said sitting down next to me.

He softly rubbed my chin and looked me in the eyes. He leaned in for a kiss. I puckered up and got ready to only be let down. He stopped midway. I opened my eyes to see what happened.

"Come on. I have more to show you," he said pulling me up.

I wondered why he stopped. Was there a woman in his life? He told me he was single. I was beginning to think I was losing my touch.

He walked me through his laundry room and out onto the patio which was furnished with a large grill, and brown wicker lawn furniture. A large pool sat in the middle of the yard. We sat on a lounging chair and took in the night's air. It was a little breezy and I didn't have a jacket. He moved in closer and wrapped his arms around me to keep me warm. I turned to him and our lips meet. We shared a few sensual pecks. When I tried to slip my tongue into his mouth, he pulled away. I jumped up in embarrassment. I didn't want him to feel like I was pressuring him into anything further, but I knew how I felt.

"I apologize," I said to him. "I don't know what came over me."

"Niyah, don't feel bad. It isn't you. You are a beautiful woman and I would love to go that extra mile with you. It is just that I want to know it isn't because you think you can get money out of me. Time after time women have tried to use me because they find out I have a huge trust fund and a nice job. I'm twenty-seven, and don't want to get involved in games of any sort. I tend to become attached after sex. So before we go too far I want us to get to know each other better."

He was upsetting me 'cause I was not a gold digger. Sure he had nice things but so did I.

"Allen, you've showed me a new me. I like the things we have done over the past few days. I enjoy the conversations we have. I don't ask anyone for anything. I do for myself and I don't like being looked upon as a whore. I thought we were getting close. I'm sorry to have taken up your time I'll leave now."

I walked off into the house and collected my things.

He didn't follow me, so I knew what that meant. This was the end of our little rendezvous. I closed the front door and walked down his driveway to my car. When I got there, I saw two red roses on my hood near the windshield wipers. I picked them up and looked around, but I didn't see him. I opened my door, but before I could get in, Allen grabbed my arm, startling me. He spun me around and kissed me. This time his tongue intruded my mouth. I felt chills and tingles all over my body. It was just a kiss, but it felt like we had just made love.

I felt so safe in his arms and I hadn't felt that way in a long time. He kissed me on the forehead, and I got in my car. We said our goodnights, and I was off.

I drove home thinking of him. I got home and took a quick shower and got in bed. The phone rang and I saw his name on the screen.

His voice was even deeper than before.

"I tried and I can't so come back now," he said in a low whisper. I didn't think twice.

I had on a long pink silk chemise. I put on my matching robe and jumped in my car and drove back out to his house. It was when I got to his door that I felt silly. I rushed over to his house in my nightclothes and what if he just wanted to talk.

He opened the door in black silk boxers. His chest was just as I imagined. He had fine curly hair on his chest and a sexy hairline leading down his stomach to his groin area. He snatched me into the door and rushed me off to his bedroom. Once inside he picked me up and placed me on his bed. He climbed on top of me and we got lost in each other's kisses. Our hands were everywhere. He slipped my gown over my head.

"I want to look at you from head to toe," he whispered.

He gazed in my eyes as he ran his fingers through my hair. He kissed, licked, and nibbled on every part of my body. He made a trail from the top of my foot to my inner thighs with his tongue. He softly blew on my clitoris, and had me speechless. He threw his boxers on the floor and slid on a condom. He took both my legs and pulled me closer. He was already on hard, so I didn't have to do anything, but lay back and enjoy the ride. He slowly inserted his penis inside until he was all the way in. But instead of moving, he just laid down directly on top of me motionless.

"What's the problem? I know you haven't cum already," I exclaimed.

"No. I wanna take you all in. You're so warm and juicy."

I wrapped my legs around his waist as we rocked to a sensual rhythm. He then laid back and pulled me on top of him. He gripped my ass and rubbed my back as I climaxed repeatedly. After a few more strokes he ejaculated. He got up and ran some hot bat water in the tub. We both bathed and fell asleep cuddling.

I was glad the next day wasn't a workday 'cause we woke up rather late. I was supposed to meet Kema at Another Broken Egg Café for breakfast. I knew she would be upset, but I would make it up to her by taking her out to lunch. I left my cell at home, so I know I had like fifty messages from her on it. I had rushed back out to return to Allen, and didn't even grab my purse. I was taking a chance of getting pulled over by the police for some dick. Well at least it was some good dick.

I told Allen my plans for the day and apologized for rushing off. He walked me to my car and kissed me on my cheek.

"Talk to you later," he asked.

"Sure thing, I said.

*I could get use to this kind of happiness,* I thought to myself as I sped off.

Chapter 28


As I walked up my steps when I arrived home, I saw Darren sitting on the top stoop. It was too early and I didn't feel like arguing with him. As I walked past him he grabbed my leg.

"You are just going to pass me up like some road kill in the street?"

I snatched away from him.

"I don't owe you shit. I don't even want to speak to you," I said.

"Niyah, look I know I fucked up again, but I need you to listen to me."

"I don't feel like going through this right now. We aren't together and never will be again so let it go. I sure have. I have moved on and I'm happy."

"I knocked on your door. Where were you last night? And why are you dressed in a night gown," he asked.

"You just don't get it do you," I asked as I unlocked my door.

The slam of my door in his face let him know I meant business.

Kema had left a message on my phone. She was whining about how I stood her up. Ariel had also left a message saying that she knew I was on a date with Allen and just wanted to know how things went. She also asked if we could do brunch or something.

I called them both and set up a lunch date at three that afternoon at Houston's restaurant. I lay down and took a nap 'til one. I quickly got dressed in some casual clothes and picked up Ariel on my way to Kema's house. I recapped my entire night and morning for her in the car. She was so happy that Allen and I hit it off.

When I pulled up in Kema's driveway I noticed Jovan's car there. I hadn't seen him in a while and really wasn't in the mood to deal with him. Just as I expected Jovan and Sandra were over. Kema told them about our afternoon arrangements and they wanted to tag along. Although I was angry, I said it was cool. Jovan was all smiles from the moment I stepped in the door. Why couldn't he play it off? Men always gave themselves away. Sandra was curling Kema's hair in the bathroom. I stepped in the kitchen to get a drink for me and Ariel out of the fridge when Jovan came in. He was all up on my ass, rubbing on it.

"What is your problem? You trying to get caught or something," I said.

I handed Ariel the glass and went to use Kema's upstairs bathroom.

A rapid knock jolted me.

"I'll be out in a minute," I said to whoever was tapping at the door.

"It's me," Jovan whispered. "Let me in."

I flung the door open.

"Are you fucking crazy? Your girl is downstairs."

"She's doing hair. That's plenty of time to savor your sweet juices."

"Get out of my way. You're sick. I should have never done it with you in the first place," I said pushing past him.

"Please," he said rubbing his semi-hard penis.

"You're pathetic," I said, walking down the steps.

I plopped on the couch next to Ariel. I whispered in her ear what happened between me and Jovan the night I showed up at his house, and what just went down in the bathroom.

"You skank," she said grinning.

Jovan eye balled me as he sat in the recliner across from us.

"Okay. Let's head out," Kema shouted.

Everyone piled into their own rides.

We all pulled up in the parking lot at the same time. I noticed Sandra checking out my car. I had driven my Infiniti Coupe.

"You like," I asked her as I trotted past clicking the alarm button. She just looked me up and down.

We were all mingling and talking amongst ourselves at the table when Jovan kept playing footsie with me under the table. I kept kicking his foot for him to stop. Every time I got up to go to the bathroom he would get up as well. He was making shit look so fucking obvious. It wasn't until we were back at Kema's house that Sandra finally put it all together.

We were sitting on the couch watching a movie on Lifetime when she jumped up pointing her finger in Jovan's face.

"It took me a while, but I got it now. How long have you been fucking Niyah? I remembered the burnt orange car that passed me in the parking lot as I came home that morning after Kema and I were out," Sandra said.

"Baby sit down. You're embarrassing yourself," he said, trying to calm her down.

"No. I left you in clothes and come back to you lying naked across our bed. I could smell a woman's perfume on my sheets. I saw the lipstick on my glass. Then today you follow and run up behind her ass all day. It wasn't until I saw the car that I realized it was her. You can't forget a color like that," she said.

I started clapping loudly.

"Bravo bitch. Fucking bravo", I yelled. "It sure took you long enough to put it all together Sherlock Holmes. So I fucked him. Who cares? You've done worse to him. He deserved to be with a real woman for one time anyway. If you had done your job and kept your man satisfied, then he wouldn't have been craving my pussy," I said.

She slowly walked up to me and put her finger in my face.

"You trifling bitch," she shouted.

"Remove your hand from my face before I break that shit for you. And a fucking breath mint wouldn't hurt your ass either," I said.

"You probably sucked his dick. That is all you're good for anyway," she snarled.

"No dear. He was the one going down on me. Don't direct your anger towards me. What you need to be doing is talking to your man."

"Fuck all of y'all," Sandra said as she grabbed her purse and stormed out.

"Let's go," I said to Ariel.

Kema couldn't close the door she was laughing so hard.

"Call me later," she yelled from the porch.

I dropped Ariel off and merged onto my exit to go home.

My cell rang.

"Hello," I snapped.

"Dang, baby. Are you okay," Allen asked.

"Oh. I'm sorry. I thought you were Kema. What's up?"

"Nothing, just missing you. I'm just chilling at the house. Why don't you stop by for a bit?"

"I'll be there in thirty minutes," I said smiling as I hung up.

# SECTION 11

## Self Intervention

Chapter 29

For weeks, Allen and I had been hanging out, and I enjoyed every minute. I knew he wasn't with me just for sex. Don't get me wrong the sex was magical, but we could sit and talk about paint on the wall and still be interested for hours on end.

The phone blaring in my ear interrupted my thoughts of him. I answered thinking it was probably Allen, without looking at the screen.

"Hi baby, how are you," I sang, into the receiver.

"Niyah this is Vince," the voice echoed loudly.

I could tell something was wrong from his tone.

"What is it," I constantly asked.

His phone was beginning to break up.

"Its Dana," he finally said over the static.

Come to find out three years ago in a random check up at her doctor's office they found a lump on one of her breast. She never told anyone and was secretly getting treated for it. She didn't reveal it 'cause she didn't want anyone to worry. They had done successful surgery and gotten rid of it, so they thought. For a few months she was in remission. She went in for another checkup a few weeks later and it was back, but in both breast this time.

She had surgery to remove them and got really sick. He said she was always tired and not able to do much nowadays. He took her to the emergency room last night 'cause she complained of a severe headache she had for the last two days.

I cried in anger 'cause she always hides things she shouldn't hide. She cared more about people getting sick from worrying over her than she did her own illness. I reassured him I was catching the next flight out in the morning to help him out and be by her side. He told me when I touch down in Atlanta to catch a cab and to meet him at the stadium 'cause he had an early morning practice and we would ride over from there.

The next morning, Ariel drove me to the airport. I caught my flight and landed in the ATL around nine. I pulled up to the stadium at about ten. The cab driver helped me out and handed me my luggage and handbags. The stadium was so quiet during the daytime. There were a few cars and trucks scattered here and there in the parking lot. There was never security on the premises while they practiced. I guess if someone was dumb enough to rob a professional football team then so be it.

All their cars and trucks tags were personalized and most people knew them when they say them on the road. I shifted my bags on my shoulder and made my way to the field. I counted steps to take my mind off of what I was really there for. I heard them yelling out on the field. I watched them some from the top balcony before walking down to the bench. They were running sprints. I sat down and crossed my legs, waiting for Vince to finish up.

I kinda missed living in the ATL. I missed the nightlife, my job, my penthouse, hell even the men I dated briefly while down.

I spotted Robert, winking in my direction as he ran by me. I looked down and noticed that most of my thigh was hanging out for all to see. Maybe I hadn't dressed properly. I had on a short form fitting black knee-length sundress with matching black tie up sandals. I shifted and tried to pull my dress down some. Just then I saw Tone running past. He looked my way, but quickly looked away when I caught his glance.

Seeing his face brought back all those memories I was trying so hard to bury. Whenever I saw his face I saw Junior's face, and I couldn't handle that. That is why I never went back when Dana would ask me to. Then I thought back on the times she would ask me to come. Was she trying to get me down there to tell me her problems? I was so selfish not to come when she needed me the most. I almost teared up again when I thought back on our childhood. I don't know how I was going to deal with seeing her lying up in a hospital bed in that state of health. She was like a sister to me and I couldn't bear losing her. Dana is one of the strongest people I knew, and for her to give in to this disease is saying a lot.

Cancer has never hit our family this close, so I didn't really know much about it. I called Sharon earlier that morning and told her what had happened to Dana. I even offered to buy her a plane ticket, so she could come and see her, but she refused, saying she couldn't take off of work on such short notice. That was just her way of not dealing with it. I called my mother during the cab ride over and told her Dana was in the hospital. She was sad to hear it and wished she were there.

I was happy my mom had found true love again. She deserved it, but I rarely saw her 'cause they traveled all the time.

A loud squealing noise interrupted my train of thought. Coach Matthews had blown his whistle to end practice. I got up to walk out to the parking lot to wait on Vince 'cause I knew they had to shower and get dressed.

"Niyah, is that you? Girl bring yourself over here," Coach Matthews yelled.

I came up to shake his hand, but he grabbed me and hugged me like I was his long lost daughter. He was an older gray-haired white man who was like a grandfather figure to everyone.

"Looking good. What brings you back here? I thought you moved away," he asked.

"I'm here on family business."

Vince said he didn't tell anyone 'cause he didn't want it to leak out to the press. That was the last thing Dana needed was cameras flashing in her face while in the hospital. Vince came over and hugged me as the rest of the team walked off. He gave me the keys to his truck and told me to go wait on him in the parking lot. He jogged off, and I walked up to the balcony where I had left my bags and went on to the parking lot. Robert caught up with me in the hall. He was panting as if he had run a mile. I frowned at him as he tried to catch his breath.

"You banging in that dress girl," he said.

I wasn't in the mood.

I left him standing there talking to himself. How dare he come up to me as if nothing happened? I know I was wrong for not letting him know we had a son together, but when he found out he still didn't come to the funeral or anything. I was so pissed with him that the only way to try to keep peace was to walk away.

I passed a few reporters in the corridor. I figured they were trying to get a story on the new trades that went down over the past few months. I must have sat there in the truck for a while 'cause I had fallen asleep. I didn't hear Vince open the door or put his things in. Tone's laughter is what woke me up. Vince was buckled in the driver's seat and Tone was leaning in the window going through a stack of CDs. I glanced in his direction, but he never even looked up at me. He handed Vince back the stack of discs and said thanks. As Vince pulled off he told Tone he would see him at the hospital. Twenty minutes later, we pulled up to Watercress Hospital. I paced myself as we walked to Dana's room from the elevator. I wanted to make sure I was ready to face the situation at hand.

Vince turned the knob and my heart skipped a beat. I saw Dana lying there with numerous tubes in her nose and arms. She didn't look like herself. Her face was pale and her eyes looked so tired. Her hair was thin and she was so skinny. I had been gone almost a year and she had drained down to nothing. She even had the nerve to muster up a smile for me. She reached her hand out for me, and I got weak in the knees. Tone was sitting in the chair near her bed, and he had to catch me from hitting the floor. I needed some air. I felt cramped in that small room.

Tone took me out in the hall.

"If I could get a drink of water I'll be alright," I said.

He walked me over to the fountain, and I took a sip. My throat felt so dry.

"You okay now," he asked.

"Yes."

When we started to walk back to the room I got body shivers. It hurt to see her like that, and I was falling apart, but I had to be there for her. I had to get my composure in tact.

Tone turned the knob and I began whimpering loudly.

"Pull yo self together," he said shaking my shoulders.

I looked up into his big, brown eyes and just let the tears fall.

"What is the matter with you," he asked.

After he saw I couldn't deal, he embraced me. He wrapped his arms tightly around my waist and held me close. I buried my face deep in his shirt and cried like a newborn baby.

"Don't worry Niyah. I won't let you go until you are ready."

I pulled away to fix myself up. I grabbed a kleenex from my purse and wiped my face. I had really messed up his button up shirt with my water works. I tried to dab the wet spots out, but it didn't seem to work. He smiled down at me as he saw what I was trying to do. He softly pushed my hands away.

"No need. I didn't really care for this shirt anyway. Tammy gave it to me."

I gave him a sharp evil look.

"I'm sorry. It seems I'm always crying in front of you," I said.

Tone understood how I felt 'cause he lost his brother. He felt my pain.

"You ready?"

"Yes," I replied.

"You sure?"

"Yeah," I said throwing the tissue away.

He grabbed me by the chin and made me look in his eyes.

"Niyah look me in the face and tell me you are fine."

"I'm cool," I stated.

He squinted and moved closer. I could feel his cool, mint-scented breath against my nose. I thought he was about to kiss me.

"Aight. You're telling the truth. I could always look deep into those beautiful eyes and tell if you were lying or not," he said.

He then made a funny face and I laughed.

He kissed me on my forehead and walked me back to the room. I hated him. He knew how to bring back all strong emotions for him I tried so hard to hide. There were a few people in the lobby smiling and looking at us. He held my hand as he pushed open the door.

"Niyah, if you feel you can't handle it then squeeze my hand and I'll take you out again."

I walked over to Dana and teared up again. She reached out for my hand. I cradled her hand in mine. She couldn't speak because of the tubes that were inserted. She just caressed the back of my hand. She tapped my thighs, and I knew she was making fun of my dress.

"Don't be hating chic, I said jokingly. "You know we have to look good no matter what."

My voice was cracking 'cause I was struggling to hold back the tears. Tone was still holding on to my hand. She pointed and smiled at us.

"What? Girl, you still trying to hook someone up? No, Dana, we aren't together. He is just here to comfort me and Vince."

She winked at me. She turned to Vince who was now sitting quietly in the corner. We all knew it was hard on him. When she made a grunting sound, he came to her side. She grabbed his hand and grabbed Tone's other hand and made them hold hands also. We all laughed 'cause she was lying on her could be deathbed and she was making jokes. She thought it was more than Tone and I was letting on to be. But she was wrong this time there was absolutely nothing between us. We sat and chatted with her for a while. It was getting late and the nurse said Dana needed her rest. We walked out to the parking lot in silence.

Vince went and pulled the truck around while Tone and I waited for him in front of the lobby entrance. I was shocked we were still holding hands. He was looking off, and I guess he never noticed he had never let it go. When Vince pulled up, Tone pulled me by my hand to get in. I stopped dead in my tracks. He looked back like what is the matter. I cleared my throat and glanced down at our hands. He caught on and quickly dropped my palm.

"I'm sorry. Forgot to let you go didn't I? I told you I would hold your hand 'til you were ready for me to let go."

He opened the passenger door and helped me up into the large truck. I brushed up against his chest as I got in.

"Can you two continue this at home? I'm hungry," Vince said.

Tone asked what we wanted to eat. Vince replied that he was craving chicken. I didn't really want chicken, and I guess the look on my face showed I didn't. Tone looked at me and asked what I had a taste for since I was frowning so. I was staring at his lips. I wanted to say you, but I said pizza instead.

"Pizza, huh? I haven't had one of those in a while. You still like veggie and pineapples?

I nodded my head yes.

"Well, you go and get settled, and I'll come over after a while and we can order in."

"Alright," I said.

He closed the door behind me.

"I'll be there in a bit. I'm gonna take a quick shower after I run a few errands."

Just then Vince's cell phone rang and he answered.

I watched Tone jog off to his truck. I don't know what happened between us, but we were back like old times. I think the ordeal at the hospital made us that way. It reminded him of when his brother died.

There were a few chicken heads pointing and gawking. Guess we gave them something to talk about. I wondered did they remember me from the baby daddy, drama on TMZ from the previous year. I waved at them as we drove off. They just snarled as usual.

*Hating ass bitches,* I thought to myself.

# Chapter 30

Vince stopped by Popeye's and got him something to eat. When we got to his place, I settled my things in the guestroom. The house was still the way Dana left it. The girl was a neat freak and it showed in every room. She was the only black person I knew that alphabetized her can goods in the pantry. I looked at the photos she had on her walls and over the fireplace. That little bighead girl just didn't know how much she meant to me. She was my shoulder when I needed to cry. My ear when I needed to vent. She was my sister and best friend in every aspect. I was going to stay there by her side for as long as she needed me to do so. I had three weeks of vacation saved up.

My phone chirped. I had four missed messages. I began checking them. My mother had called and said she got my message. She wanted to share her love and prayers with Dana and Vince. She told me to kiss Dana for her. Her and her male friend would be landing back in Memphis that upcoming Sunday. She went on about how her trip was. The next message was from Kema. She had gotten my message and gave her kind words of encouragement. She said she would see me when I returned and to call if I needed anything.

Ariel let the kids leave a message telling me that they missed and loved me. The last one was from Allen. He stated how much he wanted me to be in his arms right then 'cause he knew how sad I was about Dana. I missed him as well, but he knew I needed to be right here and he would have come to if he could have gotten off of work. Hearing his voice made me feel a little better.

The sun was beginning to set. I sat out near the pool and watched it fade away completely. Vince yelled out from the balcony did I need anything, I yelled back no that I was fine. He said he was going out with some of the boys and not to wait up on him. He told me if I got hungry to raid the fridge or the bar if I got thirsty. A few minutes later I heard him speed out of the driveway.

I had been lounging around for a few minutes and wanted to take a quick shower and change before Tone got there. I ran in and showered and just as I was about to step out to dry off when the doorbell rang.

"Shit," I shouted.

I grabbed my little silk robe to put on. Whoever it was were banging on the door and constantly ringing the doorbell, so I ran as fast as I could. I stubbed my toe on the coffee table running as I yelled out to

194

please hold on I was coming. Tone was leaning against the porch post with a wide grin on his face as I opened the door.

"You sure you happy to see me? I heard a lot of curse words coming from the other side."

"I just hurt myself," I said rubbing my foot.

"I usually have that type of affect on women."

"Boy please. Go ahead and order the pizza. I'm starved. It may take a while and I'm just hopping out of the shower."

I punched him in the shoulder as he came on in. He had a bottle of moscato in his arms. He did look rather nice in his causal attire. He had on some navy blue basketball shorts and matching Nike shirt. I could tell he had just shaven 'cause he still smelled of aftershave. I wondered why he got so spiffy just to eat pizza with me. Then I thought that he might have something to do afterward. Well I wouldn't hold him up. Right after the food was delivered I would come up with a lie and say I had a headache and rush him out. How dare he come over to spend time with me then hang with someone else afterward? I wouldn't fall into his web of lies this time. I would stop him before his game got started.

He stepped into the kitchen and picked up the phone.

"I'm placing the order. Go ahead and finish whatever you were doing."

I ran up the steps and heard him rambling in the ice bin.

"I'll fix us some drinks while we wait," he yelled up after me.

"Okay. Order some hot wings with ranch sauce also," I shouted back.

I dried myself off.

I put on my lounging pants and tank top and then put some Noxzema on my face to exfoliate my skin. I heard a glass break in the distance so I ran downstairs to see what happened. I found Tone sweeping up his mess. When he turned around and saw me he screamed.

"Hideous monster! Oh my God," he shouted as he laughed.

I rolled my eyes at him. He was so silly.

"I'm just fooling. You know you look good. Actually you look better than you have before."

"Whatever. Don't be down here tearing up my girl's house."

"I had a small accident making the drinks. I see no need in telling Vince about this mishap. Anyway the pizza and wings will be here in an hour."

My stomach was growling now. I couldn't wait sixty minutes. Well, it was a Friday night and a basketball game was on TV. Plenty of people probably ordered in. I knew Allen was glued to the tube at home.

"I'll be upstairs if you need me. Try not to break anything else."

He gave me one of his million dollar smiles and assured he wouldn't. I was in the mirror brushing my wet hair when he startled me from behind. He handed me a glass. He had poured the moscato in with a few cubes of ice and fresh cut strawberries. He also had a bag of Doritos and some cheese dip.

"Join me in the living room and we can munch while we wait."

"Okay. In a minute I'm wrapping my hair up in this bonnet."

He walked up and tied it up in the back then ran his finger down the back of my neck and it sent chills down the rest of my spine.

"I haven't touched you like this in a while," he said.

"Whose fault is that," I asked sarcastically.

He pressed himself up against me and sniffed my neck from behind. I closed my eyes and got lost in his body heat and aroma. When his lips met my left ear he whispered that I smelled good and how much he missed my soft body. I hadn't noticed his hand was on the waistband of my pants. He slipped his hand under the band and downward. But before he got to my sweet valley, the ringing of my cell broke our trance.

"I'll meet you downstairs," he said grabbing the bag of chips.

I was still standing there in the mirror dumb founded.

I picked up my phone and saw Allen's name flashing on the screen. He was at home watching the game as I predicted and he missed me and wanted to see how I was doing.

*Damn, this boy must have radar on my pussy*, I thought.

Could he have timed it any better? There ain't no telling what could have happened if he hadn't called. I told him about Dana in the hospital and that I was about to eat dinner and I would call him later.

After I hung the phone up with him, I had to go and put a cold towel on my face and neck to calm myself down. Candyland was still throbbing. I straightened myself back up and went downstairs. Tone was laying across the couch with the chips in his lap and the dip on the floor. He had kicked off his shoes like he was at home. I went into the kitchen to get down some paper plates for us to eat on. I couldn't reach them, and I guess he heard my disgust. I didn't even notice him walk up behind me. It wasn't 'til I felt him up against me that I knew he was there.

"Move, shorty, I got it. I saw you struggling and after laughing to myself I said let me help her."

I was speechless 'cause I was too into him. I was definitely feeling him if you knew what I meant. You know how when you are in the kitchen cooking and your man walk up behind you and press his body up against your butt? I could feel he was semi hard, and it made me want him more. It had been a long time since I'd felt him inside of me, and I was sure I would get that feeling back before the night was over with. He knew what he was doing. He was tall and could reach the plates, but he kept acting like he couldn't get a good grip on them. He kept pressing into me and getting harder at the same time. I couldn't handle it anymore, so I bumped him off of me and excused myself. He was playing around with me and I wasn't up for that.

I laid on the love seat and cut the TV on. I acted like I was enthralled into the game when he entered the room. He stood next to me, and I didn't look up at him. He knew I was ticked off. He sat on the couch and continued to stare at me. I could see him making silly faces in my peripheral vision. I was mad, but it was making me smile. When he saw me smile, he crawled over next to me. He leaned up against the couch. He turned to face me and licked out his tongue. I popped him in the back of his head.

Just then the doorbell rang. It was the deliveryman. Five minutes later, we were gorging out on pizza, wings, and mixed drinks.

"After this, how about a game of UNO," he asked.

"Cool with me," I replied.

I cleaned up our little mess as he set up the card game.

We sat Indian-style in the middle of the floor and played cards like little kids. We were having so much fun. On the outside looking in, you would have thought we were the perfect couple. You would have never known we went through all we did. He was such a big cheater when it came to games. I caught him hiding cards under his leg. His phone rung and it was my time to hide my cards. He turned to answer as I hide a few cards back in the deck.

"I saw that cheater," he said when he turned back around. "You're going to pay for that."

"You gotta catch me first," I said running off.

I ran through the kitchen and laundry room with him close on my heels. He almost caught me on the stairs, but I was too quick for him.

"Old man, you are getting a little slow aren't you? You know I ran track so why try to keep up with me?"

197

I hid in the linen closet 'til he ran past. I dashed out and ran back downstairs and out the back door. He was close on my tail. It was a little chilly and dark outside. We ran circles around the grill and patio furniture. I lost him when I dashed behind the bushes. He was standing by the poolside looking for me. I crept up behind him and pushed him into the pool. But to my dismay he grabbed a hold of my arm and in we both went. I was angry at first, but we started a little water fight. We were splashing around and trying to playfully drown one another. He was beginning to splash me harshly, and I got mad and climbed out.

He followed me over to the ledge asking me what was wrong.

"You're so stupid," I shouted.

"I'm sorry boo. Let me help you."

I was drenched from head to toe. He got out and got me a towel that was lying near a chair. When he came back over to me, I pushed his ass back in the water and ran upstairs. It took him a while to catch up with me. I was in the bathroom running some hot bath water. I smelled like chlorine and needed to rewash my hair. He tapped on the door and I told him I was about to take a bath and that I would catch up with him later. He said he was about to leave.

"Okay. Just pull the door up and I'll lock it later. Thanks for dinner and the game."

"Aight," he yelled back.

I took a warm bubble bath. I dried off and blow-dried my hair. I brushed my teeth and cleaned up my mess. I tied a towel around me and went to the guestroom. It was a quarter 'til ten. It was too early to go to bed. Maybe I would call Allen back and chat for a while. I ran downstairs to lock the door that Tone left pulled up. I went back upstairs and put on some deodorant and lotioned up. I stood in the mirror and tied a satin bonnet on my head. That is when Tone burst out the closet and grabbed me from behind.

Talk about your heart jumping out of your body. He had scared me good. I turned around and smacked him square in the face. He knew he was wrong for that 'cause he was grinning from ear-to-ear. He said he just wanted to get me back for pushing him in the pool the second time. I threw my brush at him and told him, I didn't appreciate that.

"Niyah, come on baby. I didn't want to leave without getting you back. I was just going to scare you when you got out of the tub, but you took so long. I went downstairs and showered in the guest bathroom and put my clothes in the washer and put on some of Vince's old college clothes and you still hadn't come out. Did I scare you?"

"Hell yeah, you did," I said as I punched him in the chest.

He grabbed my head and kissed me on my forehead.

"The poor baby. Don't worry daddy is here."

I pushed him away and that is when I noticed he didn't have anything on, but gym shorts. His chest was just the way I remembered it. He saw me checking him out. "Like what you see," he asked.

"No," I blurted as I pushed past him.

He grabbed me and spun me around to face him.

He kissed my forehead again followed by a kiss to my nose. I could feel things were starting to change with each of his kisses.

That moment was when I should have run and packed my things and caught the next flight back to Memphis.

"Can you stop that? You know what it does to me," I said.

"Tell me what it does to you," he whispered in my ear.

When our lips met, time stood still. My heart skipped a beat and I wasn't breathing. The kind of kiss you feel throughout your entire body. My arms were around his neck and his were around my waist before we knew it. His tongue was sweet like honey. He pulled away and grabbed the blanket off the bed. He held my hand as I followed him downstairs and out onto the patio. Once we were there, he slipped out of his shorts. I let the towel fall to my feet. He wrapped the blanket under him and lay back on the lounging chair.

I climbed on top of him and he wrapped the remainder of the blanket around me. Our lips met again. He shifted as his penis guided itself deep into my candyland. The wind blew over our bodies as the water in the pool rippled softly. The smell of the lilies in the flower garden enticed my senses as I rode him slowly under the moonlight in the darkness. It was peaceful and quiet except for our low moans and the light squeak of the lounging chair. He grabbed my hips as he neared his climax. After what seemed like forever, we came in unison. Exhausted, I collapsed on his chest.

He wrapped the blanket around us tighter and held me close. We drifted off to sleep in the quiet stillness of the night.

"Excuse me you two," Vince said, startling me.

It was morning. I guess we slept longer than we both expected. You tend to do that when you feel safe and comfortable and I felt that way in his arms all night.

"Don't explain. Just get inside before my neighbors complain," Vince said.

Tone and I laughed.

Vince went back inside and we wrapped in the blanket and walked together into the house. We felt a little ashamed 'cause a few of the guys were over eating breakfast in the kitchen and we had to walk past them. They just looked on in amazement. Robert just gave an angry snarl. High-fives and congrats were yelled out when we were out of sight.

I got in bed and wrapped up and shockingly, Tone joined me. I cuddled up next to him with no regrets and fell asleep. Later that afternoon I awoke to find him gone.

*How stupid of me,* I thought to myself.

This is what I got for putting myself out there. I made the goods available quick and in a hurry, and he hit it and ran.

Chapter 31

I rode with Vince back to the hospital that evening. Dana's doctor called that morning and said that Dana was getting worse. She was in desperate need of surgery, but that would be taking a chance of spreading the cancer even more. Anyway, she had talked Vince out of making her go through the procedure. She just kept repeating that she was tired and didn't want to suffer anymore. She wanted the Lord to just take her, so she could finally be at peace. I stood next to her bed and held her hand. It hurt me to tell her the lies about her mom. She missed Sharon and wondered why she wasn't there.

"She got caught up at work," I said tearing up.

That lie seemed to suffice 'cause she didn't ask about her anymore.

The next few days quickly passed by. Everyday I had Vince drop me off to visit with her while he went to practice. Tone hadn't called or come by again, and I was upset, but I didn't let it show. I shortened my trip and told Vince that I would be flying back to Memphis the next morning.

That night I had a heart-to-heart talk with Dana. We talked about old times and the people in our lives. I told her about Allen and she seemed happy to see I was finally happy. I also told her all about what Tone and I had done that previous night. She couldn't really talk, but she whispered that he still loved me. Tone had come by the night before and talked with her about me. She said he was upset with opening back up with me 'cause he didn't want to be hurt again. His way of not dealing with it was not coming back around. He didn't want to risk us getting any closer. Now, I, myself, thought that was a coward move. I had Allen, and I was not worried about Tone and his insecure issues.

Before I left with Vince that night from the hospital, I hugged Dana and kissed her head. I felt bad about going, but I was assured that we had a great talk and if anything happened to her I would be fine.

The next morning, I called a cab to pick me up from the house. I didn't want to trouble Vince anymore. I left him a note and some money to make up for me being there. During my cab ride, Vince called and asked why I left in such a hurry. I told him I needed to get back to work. I was lying 'cause I had taken off three weeks and had only stayed here a total of four days. I told Vince to call if Dana got any worse, and I would fly back down. He then said that Tone came by looking for me. I smiled a little, but I was on my way to the airport and it was too late for him to try to come and sweep me off my feet. I hung up with him and got my bags together as we pulled up to the airport. There was a slight delay with my plane. I was reading a newspaper when Tone walked up to me. We just looked at each other then I heard the voice over the speaker say that my plane was finally boarding. I got up and gathered my things.

"Tone is there something you want to say?"

He just said Niyah repeatedly, but couldn't find the other words to speak.

The voice came on over the intercom again. I turned to walk away and he grabbed my arm.

"Be careful on your flight," he said.

I frowned at him.

I knew that wasn't what he came all the way down there to say. I turned and walked quickly down toward the gate entrance. I turned around and saw him still standing there with his arm slightly extended. My seat on the plane was near the window. A tear fell as I watched the pavement of the runway as we took off.

When I landed and got my luggage I saw Allen's smiling face waiting for me outside the Memphis International Airport. I ran and hugged him like we had been away from each other for a long time.

He said Ariel told him to come and get me 'cause her smallest child was sick with a bad cold. I told him about how Dana was doing over some soup in a nearby deli. We went back to his house and made love like the first time all over again. I pushed all memories of what happened with Tone out of my mind.

Vince called me the next day and said that they discharged Dana. The doctor said she only had about two weeks to live. But Dana proved them wrong. She lived on a whole year after that. That year was the longest year of my life.

Tone sent me cards every holiday. He even had flowers delivered to my house on Valentine's Day and my birthday. I was trying my best to forget him, but he was surely making it hard for me. I would just throw his things away, I didn't feel like Allen asking about them. Allen and I were dating as of then.

Being with Allen was perfect. Everyday seemed like a new day with him. We talked on the phone or saw each other daily. Every Friday was movie night and Sunday we would take turns cooking dinner for each other. Yep this year proved to be a good one for me, 'til I got home from a club with Kema to hear a devastating message on my phone.

Dana had passed away in her sleep. I almost didn't recognize Vince's voice. I felt like such a fool. While I was out shaking my ass for all to see, Dana was dying. I felt empty and lonely. Vince decided to do a simple grave side service that upcoming Saturday. I called Vince, but I really couldn't comfort him 'cause what words can you say to comfort someone who has just lost their loved one? I didn't want him to suffer anymore, so I promised to make the calls to the family for him. I called Sharon and left a message on her phone letting her know the time and place of the funeral service. I even said I would purchase a ticket for her flight.

That night I drove over to my mom's house. We sat down and went through some old photos of Dana. I wanted to find the right one to put on the front of her obituary. We picked out some nice bible verses to print out as well. I contacted the Pastor at Dana's Church and he agreed to do her grave side ceremony. The next day on my lunch break I took everything to the local print shop and had her obituaries printed out. Her favorite flowers were lilies, so Vince bought her a head stone that had some engraved on it. He bought single lilies to hand out to the family to lie on her coffin before it was lowered in the ground.

I ordered the limos and cars to be at Vince's house at ten to pick the family up. I called almost everyone in the family to let them know the arrangements.

Saturday morning rolled around quick. Everyone had landed in Atlanta the night before. Grandma Ella and Earl, and Sharon crowded into Ella's car. They would follow behind the procession escort. Kema, Ariel, Dora, were in the second limo. Tone, Tammy, Vince, Allen, and I were in the front limo.

It was a sad day and we were all pretty much silent. It was drizzling the entire day. The services lasted about twenty minutes.

Vince completely lost it when he saw her lying in the coffin. I was glad Tone was there 'cause I could barely hold his arm up.

The family got up one by one and placed the lilies on her coffin before it was lowered into her plot. Tammy had the nerve to even cry out.

"Lord, why didn't you spare my dear friend," she shouted.

I wanted to slap her ass with my damn clutch purse, but I was a lady.

We met back up at Vince's house for dinner. People brought food by the entire week, and he ran out of room to put it, so we invited everyone to stop by and eat as much as they wanted. It was loud and stuffy in the house. I needed to get away. I sat down on the bench near Dana's lily garden and looked up at the gloomy sky. It started to rain, but it only hid my tears that trickled down. I heard mushy footsteps coming toward me, and I wiped my hair and tears from my face.

"Why are you sitting out here in the rain," the masculine voice asked.

I turned and looked up.

Tone was standing there in a black suit. His baldhead was wet from the rain. That suit accented his shoulders and arms. After I never answered him he went and stood near the pool.

"You know Niyah this isn't easy for me to say. So don't interrupt me. Hear me out entirely. Niyah, I."

Just as he was about to speak, Tammy ran out.

"I've been searching for you all over. Oh, I didn't know you were out here, Niyah. I didn't see you sitting there," she said.

When Allen rounded the corner I couldn't have been happier. He walked up to me and hugged me.

"Baby, you've been crying. Come here," he said hugging me tightly.

He slowly walked me back in the house making sure I was ready to visit with others first.

He was so compassionate. That was one of his strongest personality traits and one of the many reasons why I liked him.

I looked back and Tammy was smirking at me.

*That fake bitch,* I thought to myself.

Tone looked like one sad puppy as we walked away. He had a chance to say what was on his heart and didn't do it. I felt a little bad for walking away, but he deserved it for running out on me while I was down there previously. He'd added salt to the wound by hooking back up with Tammy.

Everyone started clearing out after a few hours. Allen, my mom, and I stayed over night to help clean up. Our flight wasn't 'til that next morning.

# SECTION 12

## Finally Moving On

Chapter 32

Our flight the next morning was at ten. That gave me enough time to go and visit Junior's gravesite. I got up about six that morning, and drove Vince's truck to the Rose Garden Cemetery. I was a little nervous 'cause I hadn't been to see him since he was buried. It hurt me too much, so I just stayed away.

Now, I had no reason to come back to the ATL. Dana and my child were gone. I had no friends here. I promised Vince I would call him to see how he was holding up. I needed to put Atlanta behind me once and for all.

I drove down the small, white pebbled pathway to where I remembered Jr.'s grave was. I had the spot marked with a willow tree. I pulled out the bouquet of white carnations from the backseat. It was about 80 degrees outside, but I felt a cold, chilly wind blow past me as I crept toward the headstone. I made sure I wore comfy clothes 'cause I wanted to sit near him and talk. I saw some baby blue roses in his cup and wondered who put them there. I figured it was Dana. She always said she visited his grave and said a prayer for him to continue to watch over me. They had begun to wither, so I pulled them out and put them in the bag I had my flowers in. I emptied the dirt clogs out of his cup and neatly placed my blossoms inside. I sat down with my back leaning up against the side of his headstone. It took me a while to find the words, but when they came they flowed.

*"Baby, please forgive mommy for all she has done. I love you and miss you so much. I lay down at night and I dream about holding you and seeing your sweet little face. I awake to see your sleepy face only to be jarred back to reality that you aren't there. Daddy loves you and always will. Never forget that. Granny loves you and talks about you all the time. You have company now, baby boy. Auntie Dana is there to hug you and kiss you and let you know everything is okay. One day we will be together forever, but until then be a good boy for mommy."*

My sentimental words were interrupted by footsteps upon the rocks on the pathway. I wiped my face and turned to see who it was. I looked up into the saddest brown eyes. It was Tone. He had a bouquet of baby blue roses in his hand.

"It was you," I said. "You're the one that leaves the flowers?"

"Yeah," he said in a low voice. "I come out here twice a month to sit with Jr."

That made me happy. Although Jr. wasn't his son, he still loved him. I got up and dusted off my pants as he placed the roses in the metal cup beside mine. I left him alone to say his words. I was placing the withered buds in the backseat when he walked up behind me. I still had tears in my eyes. He took his thumb and softly wiped them away. That same chilly wind blew between us again.

"Your flight is leaving this morning right," he asked.

"Yes, and I won't be coming back here ever again. That's why I helped Vince get things straightened with Dana's things. The memories here are too much for me to handle."

"Let me tell you something I should've told you a long time ago," he said taking my hand. "I know we haven't been on good terms over these past few years, but I wouldn't want to go through it with nobody but you. From that first day I saw you get out of your aunt's car with your bags when we were younger, I said to myself, that's gonna be my wife. You were everything I wanted. You had the body, the beauty, and the brains. You were a triple threat, and you still are."

He moved closer and kissed me. Shockingly, I didn't push him away. His sweet tongue met mines and we got lost for a few minutes, until his cell phone blared from his pocket. He looked down and put it back, and went back to kissing me. I had my arms around his neck, and he had his on my back under my sweater. My nipples were hard as diamonds. He undid my bra from behind and caressed them through my shirt. We got so carried away, we didn't even see the few cars passing by us. Then it dawned on me that we were still in the cemetery. We laughed in embarrassment as we noticed it was some funeral diggers driving by. He said to meet him at his house and I agreed.

He jumped in his truck and backed out, and I followed him.

I saw him pick up his cell and look at it a few times. I guessed it was the same person calling from before. It probably was Tammy. She was always looking for him whenever he wasn't in her face. We pulled up to his house about seven-thirty. I was pushing it, but I would get one last quickie in with him, and it would be over forever. I parked behind him in the driveway. A silver Honda Civic with dark tinted windows was parked directly across the street, but I didn't pay much mind to it at first, not until we were deep in a passionate kiss at the front door and Tammy hoped out of the car yelling at the top of her lungs.

"So this is why you couldn't come home last night, Tone? Where the hell were you in a hotel or something? Why are you hooking up with this bitch again? Why haven't you answered any of my phone calls? And don't say you didn't get them 'cause I know you did," Tammy said pointing at him.

She walked right up to him and slapped him. She never said a word to me or even turned and looked at me.

"Tammy chill the hell out. You and I aren't even dating anymore. I'm a grown ass man and can do what I want. You need to leave," he shouted.

He turned and put his keys in the lock and opened the door. He grabbed my arm to walk me in, but I was planted solid in place. A stream of tears fell as I removed his hand from my arm. I kissed him on the cheek then ran off to the truck. I backed out and didn't look back. He ran to the end of the driveway yelling out my name, but I kept on going.

This was obviously a sign that we shouldn't have been there anyway. I was tired of the drama attached to him. I got back home after eight to see Allen and my mom bringing our bags outside to put in Vince's truck. I said nothing 'cause they knew where I was. After everything was put in, Vince drove us to the airport. We all hugged before leaving. Again I promised to check up on him. I whispered in his ear for him to check on Tone 'cause I had left him in a very compromising position.

Although the flight was only forty-five minutes, it seemed like forever. When we finally landed, I was tired and wanted to go home and be alone. I fell asleep in a pool of tears on my pillow.

Chapter 33

The next four years flew by quickly. I had just turned thirty-one, and I was finally where I wanted to be in my life. My mom and her fiancé had gotten married and moved to Washington were he was originally from. Ariel and Reginald were still dating, but things were getting a little serious between them. Allen and I had gotten engaged on Valentine's Day, and our wedding was set for July of the next year.

Over the years I'd saved up a lump of money. I used it to open my own magazine franchise. It was called Corporate Divas. I had opened it two years ago and sales were through the roof. We covered articles from healthy living to mind blowing sexual experiences. Ariel was my accountant. She was good with numbers and balancing a budget. I hired Kema, as my publicist and promoter. She always had the hooks ups on parties and clubs, which would come in hand when we wanted to advertise. I was still covering all the fashion information myself. My dream had finally come true the previous year. We were on top. We were also on all the social media stages such as Twitter, Facebook, and Instagram. I would occasionally have Kema upload interview videos to our YouTube page.

One day, I was sitting in Ariel's kitchen when she jokingly said I should write a book about my life. She laughed it off, but it was a great idea. It took me only nine months to write it and it became a top seller. Who knew that people would be interested in the trial and tribulations of a black woman making it to the top?

That following winter, I was on a book-signing trip in New York. It was so cold up there, and I was looking forward to flying back to the south. I was sitting in my hotel room that Sunday before the signing. I cut on the TV and watched a football game to pass the time. The sports caster announced that a player was down and didn't seem to be moving. When he mentioned that this could be the end for Atlanta, I was glued to the screen. After the crowd around the player dispersed, I noticed it was Tone. He was lying on his back with his leg slightly bent. The replay was painful to watch. He had been hit and thrown down hard to the ground. His teammates ran over to the opposing team to start a fight, but the refs pushed them all away. I almost cried when a stretcher had to carry Tone off.

By the end of the game the analyst announced that his MRI came out positive. He had a severely torn ACL and probably wouldn't play again. He had gotten drafted right after his fourth year at LSU when he was twenty-three. He had only been in the NFL for eight years and his career was now probably over.

It was hard to hold my composure during my book signing. I kept thinking about how he was doing. Football had been his life for as long as I could remember. And I knew it was like a slap in the face to tell him he could no longer do it. I sort of wished I were there to ease his pain. Then the sight of Tammy clouded my mind, and I knew she would run and make sure her money train was okay. You know gold-diggers take care of their men when they are worth millions.

Later that night when I was back in my hotel room, I called Vince from my cell and sent my condolences to Tone. I knew how he felt 'cause I would be devastated if I injured my hands and couldn't write anymore.

After my busy weekend, I rushed back to Memphis. I was ready to get back to my normal life again.

A few months later, on the one year anniversary of my book going public, Kema threw me a surprise party. She had really kept it from me. I had been busy with a prior deadline on a fashion article, so I was always in my office. I would see her and Kema whispering to each other, but I never thought anything of it. She had rented a banquet room at Botanic Gardens. Allen had stated that he wanted to take me there and to dress nice 'cause we were going out to dinner later. He had on a nice black suit, and I had decided on a long flowing white evening gown. I felt a little funny about being dressed up, but I just figured we were going to a fancy restaurant afterwards.

The room was dark when we entered. Then the lights flew on and everyone cheered. Kema walked up and hugged me.

"Hope you're not angry," she said.

"OMG. No. Thanks," I said in awe. "You are amazing girl."

The room was beautifully decorated. Each round table had a bouquet of white roses and candles on them. They had gotten Carrabba's Italian grill to cater. A live DJ was playing soft jazz music as everyone conversed.

My mom and her husband were there as well as a few other family members, but the shock was Tone and Vince standing there. I hadn't seen Vince since the funeral, but he looked the same. He'd finally cut that beard off. Tone had a small wooden cane in his hand. I had to admit to myself he looked good as ever. Kema had invited them herself. She wanted all my friends to be there.

Jovan came up and hugged me and even Sandra did as well. I didn't want them there, but it was my night so I wasn't going to act up. Kema had gone through a lot to pull this off. We ate and danced. The night was going so perfectly that nothing could ruin it. Each of my friends stood and gave toasts to my future. Kema and Ariel just said that they were proud of me, and to make sure I never forgot them when I blew up and become mega famous and rich like Oprah.

Allen said that he was glad I was in his life and that I was a beautiful and very talented woman. My mom stood and said how she always knew I was talented since the first day she put a pencil in my hand. She told a story of how I wrote a letter to God asking him to make her better. I had a few tears in my eyes after that toast.

Sandra slammed her glass down and stood up.

"I want to say something to the famous writer," she shouted, slurring her speech. "I always knew you would make something out of yourself also. I know our friendship didn't last, but I am proud. I read your book, but I must say I was shocked to see you didn't put all the facts in it. You stated that this was a book of events in your life, yet the abortion you had when you were pregnant with Tone's baby while living at Lena's house was never mentioned. Can you explain why?"

"Liar," I screamed, crushing the glass flute in my hand, which had begun to bleed.

"It's the truth," Sandra yelled. "I was there with you."

Kema tried to hush Sandra up.

I could hear the whispers from the nearby tables. I turned my eyes to Tone and he had this look of disbelief in his eyes. Only a few seconds had passed, but it seemed like an eternity. I wish I could have disappeared at that moment. Tone stood up and slammed his hands on the table.

"All I want to know is the truth Niyah. Were you pregnant when you were at Lena's and was it mines?"

"Yes. It's all true. I was pregnant, and it was yours. But you have to understand, I was young and wasn't ready for a baby. I felt it was the best decision to make, but I regret it now. I aborted that baby and I lost a baby a few years later due to messing with a married man. And then my son died not too long ago. Is that what everyone wanted to hear? All my dirty laundry is out in the opening. Enjoy your fucking meal," I said before running outside.

Tone followed behind me.

"Why didn't you tell me," he asked.

"It was my body and my decision. I didn't want you to talk me out of getting it done."

A few tears started to stream down his cheek.

"How dare you stand here and cry Tone," I said beating his shoulder. "You never cared about me. I was easy access that's why you stayed around. I gave you the pussy with no questions asked. You strung me along then and you are trying to do it again now. I let you back into my life. And for what? To only be left standing alone. I allowed my feelings to cloud my mind again four years ago in Dana's house and you left me hanging yet again. I was saved when Tammy showed up at your house and stopped me from making another mistake."

"Don't try to make this out like you're the victim. I took in a child that wasn't even mine. I cared for that boy like he was my own. Only to be told he was someone else's. So don't tell me I didn't care. You know what? Forget it. This conversation is pointless. I'm done trying to win your heart back. I wish you all the happiness in the world. Vince told me about the engagement," he said before walking off.

I leaned against Allen's truck and sobbed.

"You alright," Allen asked running over to me.

"Take me home," I said.

That night I lay in his arms and tried to forget what happened.

Over the next ten months I pushed myself to the limit. I buried myself deep into my work. I had moved all my things into Allen's house. I hadn't talked to anyone since that horrible night at Botanic Garden. The only reason Kema and Ariel spoke with me on a daily basis is 'cause we worked together. I hadn't even talked to Vince. I just wanted to move forward finally with my life.

On occasions, my mind would wonder back to Tone and the good days we shared together. I saw photos of him and Tammy in articles at award shows. He seemed so happy and not worried about me at all. So why bother over that when I had a prince charming lying next to me night after night?

That following Friday, I had my bridal shower. It was a small intimate evening at Kema's place. My mom, Kema, and I got my last minute wedding plans together. We rented out the Columns for our wedding and reception.

Vince called and we began talking again. The night before the wedding, Kema and I decorated the entire ceremony area. We had flowers, ribbons, and candles everywhere.

After months of deciding, I finally decided on a white strapless gown that had small red crystals embedded in the train. I had my hair pinned up in ringlets. My mom hugged me and kissed me before walking down the aisle with Vince. All the guys walked in as we stood all lined up in the main hall. I peeped through the door at all our family and friends who came to see Allen and me joined in matrimony. I smiled when I saw Allen standing near the pastor in his white tux. The soft piano music played as Kema walked in followed by the other members of my bridal entourage. After the ring barrier and flower girls walked in, they made the cue for me.

One of my uncles was giving me away. I wrapped my arm into his and got ready to walk down the aisle and profess my love to my future husband. The doors slowly swung open and everyone stood to watch me march in. The loud thumping of my heart in my throat clouded out the music. Just as we were about to walk through the entranceway, Tone burst through the outside doors.

He fell down to his knees.

"Niyah, please hear me out. I've never felt this way before, and I have to make it right before you go through with this wedding. I love you and always have. When I went off to Germany I thought of you everyday. I knew one day I would find you and things would be perfect again. Although we grew apart my heart still stayed somehow tied to you. I know I may have left you hanging a few times, but know I got you now, and I plan to never let you go again. Baby, I want you to know that I can't stop thinking about you. I lay in my bed and dream of you. My soul longs to be with you. My heart beats for you. My body craves you. I need and want you in my life."

He reached in his pocket and pulled out a small box. He opened it and the most beautiful diamond ring was nestled inside.

"Will you marry me Niyah?"

I was speechless and frozen in place.

I looked down at Tone and saw the sincerity in his words. I thought back on the good times we shared as well as the bad ones. I turned and looked at Allen standing there waiting on me. Allen was my prince and shining armor and I loved him dearly. So why was it taking me so long to decide what to do? I looked at them both one more time and put my hands to my face and cried.

*What am I to do? Should I follow my heart or my mind,* I pondered.

# SECTION 13

Happily Ever After

Chapter 34

Talk about bad timing. There I was in my wedding gown ready to walk down the aisle when Tone burst in and spills his heart out to me. But I was no fool. Vince had called me a few weeks back, and told me what happened to Tammy. She and one of her fellow gold-digging friends, Amya, were at the mall shopping. The mall closed at nine and they were just walking out of Banana Republic with tons of bags in tow. They had just loaded up her new Lincoln Navigator when two young hoodlums ran up to mug them. Amya was in the passenger seat and Tammy was closing the back door when the young guy asked her to open the door. She laughed in his face and walked around to the driver's door. I guess she thought since he was so young he was playing around with her. When she hopped in the truck, he grabbed her Louis Vuitton Alma bag.

Just like the airhead she is, she fought back instead of giving up the material things. Guess nobody ever told her that material things don't compare to your own life. The other guy had pulled Amya out of the passenger seat and was taking the bags from the backseat as Tammy and the other guy fought over the purse. He even claimed to have a gun and said he'd shoot her if she didn't hand over the goods, and she still refused. She was yelling out that she worked damn hard to get the things she had. Well, she did work hard. It's tiresome giving blow jobs and laying on your back for every Tom, Dick, and Harry in Atlanta.

Amya ran off to get security as the two males dragged Tammy from the car. They grabbed her bags and purse and began to run off when she ran after them yelling for them to stop. The younger of the two pulled out a gun and aimed it right at her chest. She turned to run away and caught a bullet in the lower part of her back.

She was rushed to the hospital. Although I was happy the bitch was finally out of the picture, it was sad that she was probably paralyzed from the waist down and may be permanently be in a wheelchair.

She moved back in with her parents so they could care for her. She was no longer able to run up behind Tone and be on his arm. No wonder he came professing his undying love for me. He no longer had his bimbo.

I adored Allen, and all he did for me. He always supported whatever I choose to do. He was stable in his life even at a young age. I never encountered heartache with him, but Tone and I had a past and I did truly love him no matter what we went through. I knew we loved each other. It just seemed to be at the wrong times. When I wanted him, he was tied up with someone. Then when he realized he wanted me I was involved with someone.

We almost married once. Although he wasn't the paternal father of my son, he raised and cared for him like his own. He was even the one who placed flowers at his grave when I didn't even do so. We made the perfect couple and looked great together. I had let him slip away once. Would I let him go again?

One year later, my husband and I were sitting in the living room going through our wedding and honeymoon pictures. The wedding was straight out of a Cinderella movie. Our honeymoon was in Tokyo, Japan. We stayed at the Hotel Okura, which is centrally located in the heart of Tokyo and surrounded by exotic landscapes. We didn't rent a car. Tokyo had lots of trains and subways so we chose to travel that way to take in the all scenery.

The Hotel Okura was truly a unique place. The building had modern and traditional Japanese décor. The rooms were huge and beautifully decorated. All the restaurants we ate at were superb and offered wide ranges of different foods. The Hotel Okura also featured an extensive health club with a gym. We went in a few times during our two-week stay. At night, we would lay in each other's arms near the indoor pool. I spent my days getting full body massages and facials. One evening we shared a very intimate moment in the sauna room. There was also a traditional Japanese garden just below the Terrace Restaurant.

After dinner, we took a nice stroll through the garden. We held hands as we walked down the black and white pebbled trail way through the cherry blossom and bonsai trees. We sat on a bamboo bench and watched the moon glisten off of a pond that was filled with Koi fish.

We spent a whole day in the art and craft shops buying up décor for our bedroom. We often walked through the neighboring suburbs to the local shops. In the market place we took pictures of ancient rural temples and buildings. On our last day there we visited the Ueno Zoo. We took pictures of exotic creatures like the giant pandas and Siberian tigers, which were my favorite.

Tokyo was a beautiful place, but I was happier to spend it with the love of my life. When we arrived back home, my family said I had an aura about me. Exactly 36 weeks later, we figured what that glow was all about. My husband and I introduced our daughter, Ayani Kii` into the world. I choose that name after shopping in a shop while in Tokyo. The small Asian girl had her crystal vases on display and they caught my eye. I got her contact information just incase I wanted to purchase some more items for the office. When she stated her name was Ayani Kii`, I fell speechless. It seemed to roll off of her tongue like a soft spoken song. I asked what it meant and she said 'beautiful water'. The name stuck in my head.

Sometimes, I sit at my desk at work and look back over my life and think damn how good things turned out to be. I worked hard to get to the point I'm at now. Every night before I lay my head on my pillow I get on my knees and pray that God continues to bless me. He praised me once with the true love of my life and then again with my precious daughter, Ayani.

I had been through a lot of turmoil throughout my younger years, but I guess I needed to go through that to equal up to the woman I am today. My grandmother use to always say that God wouldn't put more on you than what you can handle. Well, he knew I was a head strong and tough spirited person and could handle everything that came my way. It was getting late. My husband placed the photo albums back on the entertainment center as I fixed Ayani's bottle and took it up to her. I rocked her in my arms and fed her 'til she fell asleep. She was only three months old, but I swore she was like a little lady. She had the curliest head of black hair and chubby cheeks. She had his nose and my hazel eyes. She was a good baby and rarely cried. I kissed her and laid her down. I went over to her dresser and pulled out a small jewelry box. I put it over in her bed and opened it. She always loved the angelic tune it played as the tiny ballerina twirled around. As I brushed my teeth and put on my pajamas, I could hear him humming softly to her. He loved her and called her his little curly top.

After I was done, I slipped into bed and cut the lamp off.

"Goodnight my princess. I love you," he said.

"I love you too my prince charming," I said, as I kissed Allen's lips.